The Registers

of

Llantrithyd, Glamorganshire.

THE

REGISTERS

OF

LLANTRITHYD,

GLAMORGANSHIRE.

CHRISTENINGS, 1597—1810; BURIALS, 1571—1810;
MARRIAGES, 1571—1752.

EDITED BY

H. SEYMOUR HUGHES.

LONDON:
MITCHELL AND HUGHES, 140 WARDOUR STREET, W.
1888.

The Registers

of

Llantrithyd, Glamorganshire.

CHRISTENINGS.

[*Several leaves at the commencement are missing*]

1597 Cissill daughter to Richard ap Res christened on ffriday the xxi of Januarie
Cissill daughter to John Deere christened on Satterday the xxij of Januarie
Wilgiffort daughter of Myryk ap Jeu^{a}n christened on ffriday the 25 of March
Jenett daughter to Richard Johnes christe'd on Tusday the xxixth of Marche
Marie daughter to James Bassett christened on ffriday the 23 of Septem

1598 Marie daughter to Wm Mathew christened on ffriday the 6 of Januarie
Cissill daughter to Thomas W^{m} christned on Wensday the xjth daye of Jann'y
Cissill daughter to Jen^{a}n D d christened on Munday the xxvijth of ffebru'ie
Cissill daughter to Thomas Warynei christened on Wensday the 5 of Aprill
Cissill David daughter to d'd Will^{a}m christened on Sunday the xxiijth of Aprill
Anthony sonn to Richard Harry christned on Wensday the xth of May
Cissill doughter to Willia' Edwa^{r}d christened a Sonday viz the xixth of November
Cissill doughter to James Bassett christened a Mvnday viz the xxth of November
Cissill doughter to Dauid Pullim christened A Twisdaye viz the xxjth of November
Anne doughter to Giles Dauid christened A Friday viz the viijth of December

1599 Anthoni sonn to Edward Jenkin christened A Thursday viz the xvth of ffebruary
James sonn to Richar ab Price christened A Saterday viz the 3 of March
John sonn to Mirick ap Jevan christened A Saterday viz the xiiijth of Aprill
.. doughter to Thomas . christened A Sonnday viz the xiijth of May
Cissill daughter to Willia' Pendry christened A Saterday viz the iiijth of August.
Susanna daughter to Richard Hugh christened A Friday viz the xvijth of August

1599 Anthoni sonn to Edward John christened A Mynday viz the xxij[th] of October.
Anthoni sonn to James Bassett christened A Wensday viz the xxj[th] of Novemb[r].
John sonn to Grifith Powell christened A ffriday viz the xxj[th] of December
Margrett Arnold the daughter of Arnold Math' of Landninood (?) was baptised the 12th of Marche

1600

John Basset the son of Tho Basset de Garne was baptised the twelft day of Aprille An'o p'cto
Elizabeth Haward the daughter of W[m] Haward was baptised 15° Aprils An'o p'dic
Margrett Harry y[e] daughter of Rich Harry was baptised y[e] five and twentith day of Aprill An'o p'd'c
Elizabeth Richard y[e] daughter of Rich Jenkin of Landinood was baptised y[e] 11th day of May
Mansell Aubrey y[e] son of M[r] Thomas Aubrey Esq[r] was bap'sed y[e] 18th day of May
Anthony Mathew the son of John Math' tayler was baptised the 8th die Nove'beris
Alis Tho the daughter of Tho ab Bevan was baptised the 12th die Septe'b'
David Howell the son of John Howell begotten on one Jane Rece and born in S[t] Hillary was baptised 1° die Dece'b'
Elizabeth Basset y[e] daughter of James Basset was baptised y[e] 10th of January
Katherin Don y[e] daughter of John Donne was baptised the 26th of ffebruary.

1601.

John Daukins } the sons of David Daukins were christened the 31th of Marcij
John Daukins } An'o p'd'cto
Mary Penry the daughter of W[m] Penry was baptised the 6th of Aprill A'o p'd'ct
Mary Myrick y[e] daughter of Myrick Eva' of Leechcastell was baptised the 14th die Maij
Willia' ffrancis the son of Mathew ffrancis was baptised y[e] 7th die of Juli An'o p'd'ct
Cissill Daukin the daughter of George Daukin was baptised the 25th of August An'o p'd'cto
Margret Haward the daughter of Rice Haward was baptised the eaight day of December An'o p'd cto
John Nicholl the son of John Nicholl was baptised the 27th of ffebruarij An'o p'to.

1602

Mary Awbrey the daughter of Thomas Awbrey Esq[r] was baptised the 11th day of Aprill An'o p'cto
Jenkine Richard the son of Richard Rice of the p'ish of Lancarvan was baptised in the church of Lantrythid the thier day of Julij An o p'dict
Mary Daukin the daughter of David Daukin was baptised the 21th day of Julij An'o p'dicto
John Basset the son of James Basset was baptised the fourth day of September.
Jane Mathew the base daughter of Morga' Mathew begotten one the body of Mary ffabia' was christened the eaightene day of September
Alis Dere the daughter of John Dere was baptised the third of November
Elizabeth Mathew and Catherin Mathew the daughters of John Mathew tayler was baptized the eaight day of Januarij
Joan Earle the daughter of Phillip Earle borne in Leech Castell was baptized the eaight day of Januarij
Anthony Haward the son of Rice Haward was baptized the seventh of March
Anthony Thomas borne in Landinoud the son of Tho John Mellin of the sayd p'ish was baptized the 14 of March

1603

Elizabeth Niccholl the daughter of John Niccholl was baptized the 26th of March
Mary Harry the daughter of Richard Harry was baptized the 14th Aprilis
Katherin David the daughter of David Willia' was baptized the 22th Maij
Katherin Edwards the daughter of Willia' Edwards was baptized the first day of Julij
John ffrancis the son of Mathew ffrancis was baptized the eaight of Julij
Margret Dawkin the daughter of David Dawkin was baptized the 23th of September
Ann Charles the daughter of one Charles borne in Leechcastell was baptized the 2^{d} of Octob'
Joan Basset the daughter of Thomas Basset was baptized the 12th of October
Elizabeth Yeavan the daughter of Roger Yeava was baptized the 17th of Dece'b'
Cissill Morga' the daughter of Rece Morga was baptized the 12th of Februarij
Joan Thomas the daughter of Thomas ap Evan was baptized the 15 of Februarij

1604

Anthonie Penry the son of William Penry was baptized the 27th day of Octob' An o p'd'c'o
Richard Basset the son of James Basset was baptized the first day of Decemb
An Piere the daughter of Morga' Piere was baptized the eaght day of Decemb'
Christian Matho the daughter of Thomas Matho was baptized the first of Febru'
Elizabeth Gwine the daughter of John Gwine de garne was baptized the 23th Februarij
John Awbrey the son of Thomas Awbrey Esq was baptized the 24th Frebruarij

1605

Margret Mathew the daughter of John Mathew tayler was baptized the 25th May
Elizab Rosser the daughter of Mathew Rosser was bapt 23th Junij
Elizab Basset the daughter of John Basset of Borastown was baptized ye 28th Junij
Ginnet Haward the daughter of Rece Haward was baptized the 7th of Octob'
Joan Penry the daughter of Harry Penry was baptized 17th of Novemb
Anthonye Mathew the son of Morgan Mathew was baptized the 15 of Januarij.
Thomas Basset the son of James Basset was baptized the 31th of Januarij

1606

James David the son of David Willia' was bapt the 17th of Aprill An'o p'd'ct.
Ann Rosser the daughter of Roger Evan was bapt the 19 of Aprill An'o p'dict
Hughe the son of Mathew ffrancis was baptized the first of Maij An'o p'dict
Nest the daughter of John Robert Aprice borne in Lansinnfred in Gwenbuge (?) Moore in Munmuthshere was bapt in the church of Lantytreed 6 die Junij An'o p'd'ct
Anthony Dawkin the son of D'd Dawkin was bapt the seaventh day of Julij An'o p'd'ct
Margrett the daughter of John Mathew taylor was bapt the 10 of Julij An'o p dict
Katherin the daughter of Mathew Rosser was bapt the 26 of Octob
Elizabeth the daughter of Rich Thomas of Leechcastell was bapt 1° die Nove'b'
W^{m} son to Morgan Haward was baptizsed the 15 day of Dece'b'
ffrancis the daughter of Wm Haward was baptized the 31th Dece'b'
Blanch the daughter of James Basset was bapt 12 Januarij
David the son of Thomas Dawkin was bapt 14 Marcij

1607

Mary the daughter of Morgan Mathew was bapt 28 Marcij
Thomas the son of Henry Penry was baptized the 14 of May

John the son of Anthony Gwin Esq was bapt the 28th May
Elizabeth the daughter of Wm Penry was bapt 29 Maij
Jane the daughter of Lewis Dawkin was baptized 14 Junij
Elizab Prichard the daughter of Edw Prichard was bapt. the sixt day of August
Elizab the daughter of Wm Dawkin was bapt the 16 day of August
Ann the daughter of Tho Basset de garne was bapt the 13 of Sept
Margret the daughter of Morga' apreece was bapt the 15 of Nove b'
William the son of Reece Haward was bapt the 7th of Januarij
Ann the daughter of George Dawkin was bapt the 9th of Januarij.
John son of David Dawkin was baptised 7° Februarij
Barbara the daughter of James Basset was baptised . . of Februarij

1608

Harry the son of Roger Piere (?) was baptized the second of Aprill
Thomas Awbrey son to Thomas Awbrey Esqr was bapt the 21 of Aprill
An the daughter of Matho Rosser was bapt ye 22th of May
Elizab the daughter of Thomas Dawkin was bapt 1° die Junij
Mary Penry the daughter of Henry Penry was bapt 18 of June An'o p'dict
Barbara daughter of John David of p'ish of Newcastell was bapt 22th Julij
Thomas the son of Anthony Gwin' Esqr was bapt 18 day of Sept'
Katherin the daughter of Richard Thomas of Leechcastell was bapt the 29 day of Sept'b'
Rece the son of Morgan Yeava' was bapt 6° die Octob'.
Elizab the daughter of Mathew ffrancis was bapt 22do die Januarij

1609

Christofer the son of James Basset was bapt. 14th of Aprill
Ann the daughter of Morgan Haward was bapt 3° die Junij
Mary the daughter of Edward Jenkin was bapt ye 16th die of June
Katherin the daughter of Henry Penry was bapt ye 19th of August
An the daughter of John Matho tayler was bapt die Februarij

1610.

John Gwin the son of Anthonie Gwin Esqr was bapt ye 4th of Maye
Cissill the daughter of Roger Lewis was bapt the 3° dey of June
Christian Prichard the daughter of Edw Prichard was bapt 18 Julij
Elizab Haward the daughter of Rice Haward was bapt. 14th August.
Christoffer the son of Wm Daukin was bapt. 26 of May
William the son of Mathew Rosser was bapt 16 of Sept
James the son of James Bassett was [bapt] the 23 of Januarij
Jane the daughter of Richard Adam was bapt 26 Januarij
James the son of Morgan Aprecce was bapt 27 Januarij

1611.

Katherin the daughter of Wm Bersey was bapt octavo die Julij
Maria Prichard fillia Ed'r's Prichard baptizata erat 27° Junij
Mathew the son of Wm Matho was bapt 26 of Octob'
An the daughter of Edward Jenkin was bapt 23 of Nove'b'
Cissill the daughter of Wm Thomas 1 ffrebrui
Alic the daughter of Matho ffrancis was bapt 28th ffrebruarij

1612

John the son of Morga' Yeavan was bapt. 14 of Maij
Maria filia Anthonij Gwin Armig baptizabatur 8° die Novembris.

John Penrye the sonne of Henrye Penrye was baptized 24 Novembris
William Basset the son'e of James Basset was baptized 28 Novembris
ffrauncis the son'e of Mathew Rosser was baptized the 29 Novembris.
Godwin Prichard the son' of Edw Prichard was bapt 23 of March

1613

Morgan Haward the son of Rice Haward was bapt. 1° die Aprilis
Edward the son of Thomas Jenkin was bapt 3° Junij
ffrisw^th^ the daughter of Richard Adams was bapt 16 of June
Jenkin the son of Wm Daukin was bapt 21 Junij
Gwenllian the daughter of Wm Morga Esqr Thomas Awbrey his brwer was bapt 7° Augustij
George the son of Morgan Haward was bapt 22° Octob'
Edward the son of Rosser Lewis was bapt xj° Marcij
Thomas Gwin the son of Anthony Gwyn Esqr was bapt 8° Marcij

1614

An the daughter of James Bassett was bapt 13 Junij
Ann the daughter of Wm Haward was bapt 2° die Octob'
An' the daughter of Edward Prichard was bapt 2do die Marcij
Anthony the son of Anthony Gwin Esqr was bapt 23° Marcij

1615.

Mathew the son of Mathew Francis was bapt 14 Aprilis
Anthony the son of Edward Jenkin was bapt 2do Aprilis
Joan the daughter of Tho Younge was bapt 13° Decemb'
Joan the daughter of Roger Aprece was bapt 10 Februarij
George the son of Rice Haward was [*remainder of entry quite gone*]
Richard the son of Jenkin Willia' was bapt 1° die Marcij

1616.

Thomas son of Mr David Jenkins was bapt 7° die Aprilis
An the daughter of Richard Adam was bapt 16 Maij
Mary daughter of Robert Buttn [*sic*] gent was bapt 13 Julij
An daughter of Thomas Jenkin was bapt 11 die Augustij
John the base son of David Powell Clerk and Cuiatt of Monke-Nash was bapt 16 of Septemb
Ginnet the daughter of Thomas Daukin was bapt 21 Dece'b'
Charles the son of James Basset was bapt 29 Decemb.
Mary the daughter of Willia' Mathew was bapt 1° Januarij
Myricke the son of Roger Lewis was bapt 11 Jann^a^rij
Christian the daughter of Edward Jenkin was bapt 24 Januarij
Alicia filia Ed Prichard rect' baptizabatur 17° die ffebruarij

1617

Margrett and Joan the daughters of John ap John deceassed were bapt 2 Maij
Mary the daughter of Mr David Jenkin was bapt. 24 Aprilis.
Ginnett the daughter of Thomas Yon'ge was bapt 8° Februarij
An the daughter of Mathew Francis was bapt 1° Marcij.

1618

Philemon filius Edwardi Prichard baptizatus erat 20 Maij
Edward the son of Thomas Jenkin was bapt 17 of Jann^u^rij

1619

An the daughter of Thomas Younge was bapt 21 May
Anthony the son of Richard Adam was bapt 1° die Junij
Gynnett the daughter of was bapt[sd] secu'do Decemb
John the son of Rice Haward was bapt. 25 ffebru[a]ry

1620

Rice the son of W[m] Mathew was bapt. the 22[th] of Aprill
Katherin the daughter of David Jenkins Esq[r] was bapt the 23[th] of Aprill.
John the son of Howell John was bapt 28° Maij
Aliciam filia Edw Prichard baptizat' 22° Julij
William the son of John Bassett de garne was bapt. 3° die Novemb'
An the daughter of Morgan Thomas was bapt 14 Martij
Gynnet the daughter of Mathew ffrancis was bapt 18° Martij

1621.

Margrett the daughter of Roger Lewis was bapt 2[do] Aprilis
William y[e] son of Thomas Jenkin was bapt 16 Maij
Willia' the son of Morgan Yeava' was bapt the ninth of ffebru'
Katherin the daughter of Morga' John was bapt[d] 23° ffebru'.
Lewis the son of David Jenkins Esq was bapt[d] 21° Ma tij

1622

An' the daughter of W[m] Hu'llin was bapt decimo Aprilis
Magdalena filia Edw Prichard baptizabatur 23° Aprilis.
Mansfeild y[e] son of John Bassett bapt 20 Maij
An' the daughter of Rice Haward was bapt 3° die Julij

1623.

An' y[e] daughter of David Jenkins Esq[r] was bapt 6 Aprilis
Jenkin the son of W[m] Matho was bapt 15° Aprilis
Mary the base daughter of Mathew ffran'cis was bapt 26° of Julij
William the base son of Thomas Hullin was bapt[d] y[e] 15° of Novemb.

1624.

Elizabeth the daughter of Thomas Jenkin was baptised 24 Augustij
John the son of Morgan John was bapt [*month omitted*]
David y[e] son of William Hullin was bapt. 3° Octobris.

1625.

Marke the son of John Rees was bapt 23° Aprilis
Jane the daughter of David Jenkins Esq[r] was bapt 4[to] Sept
Joan the daughter of William L llin was baptized 22° Jann[a]rij
Tabitha the daughter of Edward Prichard was bapt 31 Maij

1626

Katherin the daughter of Edward W[m] de Burthin was bapt 14° Maij
Mary the daughter of David Jenkins Esq[r] was bapt 3° Septemb'

CHRISTENINGS

1627.

Thomas the son of Morgan John was bapt 11° Maij
Morgan the son of Robert Thomas was bapt 28° Julij
Elizabeth the daughter of David Jenkins Esqr was baptized 2° Septemb'

1628

Anthony the son of Wm Hullin was bapt 2° Julij
Anthony the son of Robert Thomas bapt 6° Julij.
Henry the son of Thomas Mathew was bapt decimo septimo Novemb'

1629

Mary the daughter of Water Baskersvill was bapt 8 Octob'
Cissill the daughter of David Jenkins Esqr was bapt 26th of November
Edward the son of Robert Thomas was bapt 19th of Decemb'

1630.

Thomas the son of Thomas Mathew was bapt 26° Junij
William the son of Morgan John was bapt decimo septim° Julij
Richard the son of Thomas Love was bapt 22° Augustij
Elizab the daughter of Walter Baskervill Esq was bapt 26° of Septemb'
William the son of David Jenkins Esqr was bapt 28° Novemb'

1631

Marie the daughter of Thomas Penrie was bapt 8° Maij
Maria filia Johannis Awbrey Arm baptizabatur septimo die Augustij
Ann the daughter of Rice Walkin was bapt the eaighteenth of Septem'
. the daughter of John Rees was bapt 20 Maij
William the son of Harrie Robert was bapt 4° Decemb
Thomas the son of Thomas Love was bapt 29° Jann^rij.
Cissill the daughter of Walter Baskervill Esqr was bapt 13° M'cij

1632

ffrancis the son of Robert Thomas was baptised 7° die Aprilis
Elizabeth the daughter of Thomas Penry was baptized the xiij^th day of May
Joan the daughter of Thomas Penrie was bapt the 17° of Febru'
Mathew the sonne of was bapt M'cij
Ann the daughter of Jenkin Thomas was bapt 22° M'cij
Katherin the daughter of Rice Walkin (or Wilkin) was bapt 24° M'cij

1633.

Cissil the daughter of Harrie Robert was bapt 20 Maij
Ludovicus filius Johannis Awbrey Armigeri baptizabatur undecimo die Augusti
Rice the son of Morgan John was bapt 15 8bris
Ann the daughter of John Harrie was baptised 15 Marcij
Marie the daughter of John Matho was baptised 24 Marcij

1634.

Margrett the daughter of William Hullin was bapt 13° Aprilis
John the son of John Rees was bapt 3° Maij
Ann the daughter of Watkin [*sic*] was bapt septimo Octob'

1635.

Ann the daughter of Morga' Jen^a^n was bapt 22° Marcij
John the son of Jenkin Thomas was baptised 10 Septemb'
Cissel the daughter of Wm John was bapt. 12 Octob'.
Philemon the sonne of John Matho was bapt 11° Octob'
Katherin the daughter of Jen^a^n Jenkin of Llanfey was bapt 20 Jann^a^rij 1634 [sic]
Jane the daughter of Robert Thomas & Mary his wife was babtized the 1^t^ day of May 1640 [sic]
Gynnett the base daughter of W^m^ as the mother called . . affurmeth was bapt 30 die Jann^a^rij
Jane the daughter of John Harrie was bapt 2° Febru.
Morgan the son of Morgan John was bapt 30 Jann^a^ry

1636

Tho the sonn of Harrye Robert and Cissell Penry his wife was bapt 11 Junij
Katherin and Mary the daughters of Robert Thomas and Mary Tho his wife were bapt. 21 Junij
Lanncl'ott ye base sonn of William Mathew begotten on ye body of Anne Mathewe was bapt 8° Septemb'
Thomas ye sonn of Anthony Roggers and Ann John his wife was baptized 21th of Septemb'.
Rebecka the daughter of Watkin Dauid and Katherin Beesie (?) was bapt 1° Octob'
Elizabeth the daughter of Wm John and Katherin Edward was bapt 4° Decemb'
An' the daughter of William Hullin and An' Harris his wiffe was bapt 25° Decemb'
Jane the daughter of Morgan Jen^a^n and An' John his wiffe was bapt 10 Febr

1637

Maximilia' the son of Jenkin Thomas and Elizab George his wiffe was bapt 25 Marcij
Jane the daughter of John Matho and Margrett his wiffe was bapt 1° Aprilis
Elizabetha filia Johannis Awbrey Armigeri et Maria eius vxoris baptizabatur 2° Julij
Maria filia Thomæ Awbrey in legibus Bacchalaurij et Elenoriæ vxoris eius baptizabatur 3° Novembris

1638

Alicia filia Tho ap Tho et Annæ Prichard eius vxoris baptiz 21 Aprilis
Gwilhelmus filius Johanis Harrie (' Harris) et Marsleiæ vxoris eius bapt vltimo die Junij

Maria nata Johannis Henrici et Marsleriæ eius uxoris in lucem hanc proficiscitur quindecimo die Maij Anno Dom' 1644 *

Cisalia filia Johan'is Awbrey Armigeri et Mariæ vxoris bapt. vigessimo 2do Julij 1638
the son of John Rees and his wiffe was bapt 26° Octob' 1638.
W^m^ the base son of Phillip Leonord and Katherin Dawkins was baptised vltimo Novemb' 1638

William the son of Thomas Awbrey gent and Elinor his wiffe was baptised the fowrth daie of November An'o D'ni 1640 †
Elizabeth the daughter of Sr John Awbrey Knight and Barronett and the lady Marie Awbrey was baptized the thre and twentith daie of May An'o D'ni 1645.
Johane the daughter of Phillipp Robertes and Ann his wiffe was baptized the twentith of December An'o D'ni 1647

* This entry inserted in the margin † Dates irregular in original

Anthony the sonne of William Howard & Wenllyan his wife was borne on Monday the four and twentith of June 1644

Jenett the daughter of William Howard & Wenllyan his wife was borne on Wednesday the xvijth of September 16 [*defaced in original*]

Christopher ye sonne of Jenkin Dawkin was baptized the third of October 1651

Joan ye daughter of Philip Robert baptised the 31th of August 1653

Joan ye daughter of Benjamin Layton baptised Decemb' 15th 1653

Elizabeth ye daughter of Richard Bassett of Garne baptized ye fift of January 1653

Joan ye daughter of Tho Jenkin was baptized 30th of July 1654

Evan ye son of Lewis Gronow baptized ffebr' 7th 1654

Jo^{n} ye son of Jenkin Dawkin baptized ffebr 18th 1654

James the sonne of Jo^{n} Bassett was borne the two and twentith day of November 1642

Katherin the daughter of Jo^{n} Bassett was borne the 14th of Aprill 1644

Thomas the sonne of Jo^{n} Bassett was borne the xiiijth of May 1646

Ann the daughter of Richard Bassett and was baptized December the ninth 1648 *

Anne the daughter of William Morgan was baptized the 2 day of ffebruary 1660

Jenking Thomas Wass prone the 2 day of May 1661 †

Ciscill the daughter of Thomas Powell was baptized the 17th day of August 1664.

Ciscill the daughter of Robart Watkin was baptized the 10th of January 1664

Gwillim the sonne of James Hugh was baptized the 14th day of ffebruary 1665

Gorge the sonne of Gorge Jenkin was baptized the 4th day of March 1665

William the sonne of a strange woman was baptized the 18th day of August 1667

Mary the daughter of Thomas Powell was baptized the 8th day of September 1667

Mary the daughter of John the miller was baptized the third day of May 1668

Ciscill the daughter of James Hugh was baptized the 6th day of March 1669

John the sonne of William John of this parish was baptized the 23th of Aprill 1670

John the son' of Will John of this p'ish was baptized the 29th of January 1670

Will ye son' of Will John of this p'ish was baptized ye 10th of June 1671

Thomas the son of William John was babtised the 12 of January 1671

Ann the daughter of Will Anthony was babt^{d} ye 26 of March 1672

Georg the son of Watkin David was babtized the 11th of December 1672

Robert ye son of Jon Robert and Jane his wiffe was babtisd ye 21th of Nouember 1675

Thomas ye son of Petter Leonard and Anne his wife was baptized ye 23th of 9^{ber} 1678

Florence the daughter of Charles Howard was babtized the 29th of August An'o 1672.

Lettice the daughter of Charles Howard was babtized the 14 of November Anno 1677

Margery ye daughter of William John & Catherin his wife was babtized May ye 29 1679

William ye son of John Cortney babtized ye 15 of August 1679

Morgan ye son of Isacke Dauid was babtized ye 5 of 9^{ber} 1679

Elenor ye daughter of Watkin Dauid babtizd 9^{ber} ye 15 1679

Cissill the daughter of Thomas Rosser was babtized October the 2^{d} 1680.

William the son of Christopher Dawkin was babtized ye fifth day of March 1679

John the son of Sr John Awbrey Bar^{nt} was babtized the 27 of May 1680.

Mary ye daughter of Peter Leonard & Anne his wife was babtizd Feb 2^{d} 1680

1681

Richard ye son of Thomas Morgon was babtized May ye 7th

Jane ye daughter of Anthony Reece & Elizabeth his wife was babtiz' ye 19 day of May

Mary (Cissell *erased*) the daughter of George Rosser & Elizabeth his wife was baptised ye 16th day of 8^{ber}

* Occurs among the Burials † Occurs on a page at end of the Register

1682.

Reese the son of Wm John and Cathrein his wife was baptiz' ye 2th of November
Floranc ye daughter of Charls Morgan was baptiz' ye 20th of Dec.
Joan ye daughter of Wm Hopkin was bapt' Jone [*sic*] ye 12th
Mary the daughter of Christopher Daukin was bapt' Des' ye 27th
George the son of Richard John was borne the 20 of November
Alis ye daughter of Watkin David was baptised ye 31 of December.
John ye son of Lewelin Morgan was baptized ye 2 of February.
Henry ye son of Isack David was baptized ye 10 of Janvary.

1683

James the son of Edward James was baptized ye 12 day of August
John ye son of Tho. Rosser was baptized ye 16 of August.
Richard the son of Charles Morgan was baptized ye 2d of November
Nathaniell the son of William Mathew was baptized the 16 of June
Thomas the son of Thomas Morgan was baptized the 30 of December
Richard the son of William Hopkin was baptized 12 of March

1684

Philemon the son of Lewelin Morgan was baptized ye 16 of June.
Anne ye daughter of Christopher Thomas was baptized ye 11 of August
Miles ye son of Christopher Daughkin was baptized ye 21 of August
Mary ye daughter of Christopher Sypia was baptized ye 17 of November.

1685

Mary ye daughter of Samvell Coale was baptized ye 21 of Aprill.
Kate the daughter of Isaac David was babtized the 17th of May
Edward the son of John Courtney was babtized the 28 of May
Morgan the son of John Christopher was babtized the 7th day of June being Whitsunday
Thomas the son of George Rosser was babtized the 21 day of June
Thomas the son of Christopher Thomas was babtized October 15
John the son of William Mathew was babtized October the 18
John ye son of Samuell Coale was babtized February the 21.
Thomas ye son of Watkin David was babtized March 14 being Sunday

1686

Cecill ye daughter of John Davis was babtised ye 28 of March being Sunday
Jenkin ye son of Christopher Dawkin & Ann his wife was babtised ye 6 of Aprill
Hopkin ye son of William Hopkin was babtised ye 2d day of May
Joan ye daughter of Anthony ye gardiner was babtised ye 19th of September
John ye son of Mr William Basset of ye Garn and his wife was babtised ye 20th day of Decem'
Lewelin ye son of Richard John was babtised [*no date given*]

1687

Catherine ye daughter of Llewelin Morgan was babtised ye first day of May
Samuell the son of Samuell Cole and Ellenor his wife was babtised the 4th of December
the daughter of John Christopher was babtised the 26 day of December
Thomas the son of Mr William Bassett of the Garn was babtised Febr' 27

1688

John the son of Hopkin Jenkin was babtised the tenth day of May
Magdalen the daughter of Christopher Dawkin was babtised September the ninth
Thomas the son of Charles Morgan was babtised the twenty second day of September
Richard the son of Christopher Scipio was babtised the seaventh day of October
William the son of Anthony William Gardiner was babtised the tenth day of October
Katherine the daughter of William Hopkin was babtised the 28 of October
William the son of Edward James was babtised the 16 of November
Catherine ye daughter of John Griffith was babtised ye 27th of December

1689

Mathew the son of Watkin David was babtised on Easter Monday
. the son of John Christor was babtised ye 7th of July
Thomas the son of Anthony Morgan was babtised the 11th of October
Thomas the son of Llewelin Morgan was babtised ye 22^d of December

1690.

Jennett the daughter of Isaac David & Catherine his wife was babtised Aprill 27.
Christopher the son of Mr Christopher Thomas was baptized May 28th
John the son of Anthony William Gardner & Joan his wife was babtised November 1st.
David ye son of Llewelin Andrew was babtised ye 16th of November.
William and Jennet twinns ye son and daughter of Watkin David were babtisd Nov 24th.
Ann ye daughter of Christopher Dawkin was babt' Dec 7
Ellenor ye daughter of John Christor was babt' Jan 28

1691

John ye son of Charles Morgan was babtis' May 3^d
George ye son of Hopkin Jenkin was babtised ye 21 of June
Joan ye daughter of Anthony Rees was babtised ye 4th day of September.
Kate ye daughter of Watkin David was babtised ye 15th day of November

1692.

Mary ye daughter of Mr Christopher Thomas was babtised Nov 21
Catherin ye daughter of Anthony William Gardner was babtised Dec 18
Jenkin the son of Christopher Dawkin was babtised Jan 6
George ye son of Rees Nicholas & Elizabeth his wife was babt' Jan 19.
Phillip the son of Anthony Rees was babtised on Candlemas-day.
John ye son of Lewis Howell was babtised Febru' ye 5

1693

Mary ye daughter of Edward James was babtised on Lady-day

1694

Ann ye daughter of John Christor was babtised Oct 15.
Mary ye daughter of John Wilkin was babtised Nov 6.

1695

Thomas ye son of Robert Howell was babtised Aprill ye 6th
Robert ye son [of] Rees Nicholas was babtised Aprill 9th

Margarett the daughter of William Thomas & Mary his wife was born June 10th & christn'd June 13th
George ye son of Charles Morgan & Mary his wife was born September ye 2d & christn'd September ye 8th
Mary ye base daughter of one Mary Lewis of ye parish of Lancarvan was born ye 14 & christned ye 15 of September
Curl ye son of Anthony William & Joan his wife was born ye 22 & babtised ye 25 of October
John ye son of George Rosser & Elizabeth his wife was born ye 27 of October & christn'd ye 7th of November
Tabitha ye daughter of Anth Morgan & Elizabeth his wife was born ye 27th & christn'd ye 30th of January

1696

Margaret ye daughter of Lewis Howel & Ann his wife was born ye 11 of Aprill (being Easter Day) & christn'd Aprill 19th
Reece ye son of William Thomas & Mary his wife was born ye 11th & christned ye 14th of March
George ye son of George Rosser & Elizabeth his wife was born ye 18 & xned ye 25 of March

1697

Elizabeth ye daughter of Christopher Dawkin & Ann his wife was born ye 9th & xned ye 13th of May
Robert ye son of Rhoderick William of Penmark & Lettice his wife was born ye 7th & xn'd ye 27th of June
Mathew ye son of William Thomas & Elizabeth his wife was born ye 18th & xnd ye 29th of August
Thomas ye son of Anthony William & Joan his wife was born ye 29th of 7ber & xn'd ye 4th of 8ber
Benjamin ye son & Elizabeth ye daughter of John Wilkin & Jane his wife were born ye 1st & xnd ye 3d of November
Mary ye daughter of John Courtney junior & Katherin his wife was born ye 15 & babtised ye 19 of December
Margaret ye daughter of Richard John jun & Lydia his wife was born ye 23 & xnd ye 30 of January
Mary ye daughter of Robert Howel & Bridget his wife was born ye 2d & xnd ye 6th of February

1698

Morgan ye son of Charles Morgan & Mary his wife was xnd ye third of August
Ann ye daughter of John Thomas & Ann his wife was christned Sept 21
Mary ye daughter of William Thomas labourer & Elizabeth his wife was xnd Febr 3

1699.

John ye son of John Covrtney was xnd the 3d of 7ber
Margaret ye daughter of Richard John & Lydia his wife was xnd the 10th of 8ber

1699-1700

Anne the daughter of Jn Wilkins was xtnd the 11 of Feb

1700

John and Jane the son and daughter of William Thomas were xtnd ye 7 of Aprill
the daughter of John Christopher was xtnd the 13th of Aprill

Margarett the daughter of Tho Howell was xtned ye 10 of May
Elizabeth the daughter of Jn Courtney was xtened the 30th of 7ber
Evan the son [of] Watkin David was xtened the 16 of 8ber
Mary the daughter of William Watkin was xtened the 20th of November

1700-1

Evan the son of Anthony William was xtened the 30th of January
Robert the son of Robert Howell was xtened the 23 of February
Thomas the son of William Thomas was xtened the 23 of February

1701

Thomas the son of Richard John was xtened the 1 of June
John the son of Gwilime Hugh was xtened the 7 of August
Jennet the daughter of Evan Morgan was xtened the 28th of 7ber

1702

Thomas the son of William Watkin was xtened the 28 of March
Jane the daughter of Anthony William was xtened the 15th of Aprill
Margarett the daughter of Sr John Aubrey Bartt was xtened the 5th of May
Morgan the son of John Courtney was xtened the 11 of October
Edward the son of William Thomas was xtened the 30th of October
Margarett the daughter of Gwilime Hugh was xtened the 11 of 10ber.

1702-3

William the son of John Wilkin was xtened the 10th of January
Anne the daughter of Thomas Roberts was xtened the 27th of January

1703

Jane the daughter of Richard John was xtened the 25th of July
Mary the daughter of Sr Jon Aubrey Bartt was xtened the 26th of August

1703-4

Elizabeth the daughter of William Courtney was xtened the 26th of January

1704

William the son of Wm Thomas was xtened the 6th of August
Anthony the son of Anthony William was xtened the 27 of August
Jane the daughter of Sr John Aubrey Bartt was xtened the 21 of October.
Elizabeth the daughter of Rob Howell was xtened the 29th of 9ber
Mary the daughter of Tho Roberts was xtened the 1st of Feb

1705.

Cissil the daughter of Gwilim Hugh was xtened the 3d of October.
Cissil the daughter of Sr Jon Aubrey Bartt was xtened the 29th of 9ber

1706

Charles the son of William Thomas xtened the 6th of October
William the son of John Courtney was xtened the 24th of 9ber

1706-7

John the son of Sr John Aubrey Bartt was born the 2d of January and xtened the 23d of Jan
Mary the daughter of Thomas Roberts was xtened the 27th of Feb
William the son of Richard John was xtened the 8th of March 1706 [*sic*]

1707.

Edward the son of John William was xtened the third of 9ber

1707-8

Elizabeth the daughter of Gwilime* was xtened the 18th of Feb

1708

Lewis the son of Robert Howell was xtned the 1rst of Aprill
Mary the daughter of Wm Courtney was xtned the 25 of Aprill
Rees ye base son of David Scipio baptis'd ye 18th day of May
Thomas filius Joh'is Aubrey Bartti natus 29° die Maij baptisatus 14° die Junij

1708-9

Elizabeth the daughter of Thomas Roberts baptized the 23rd day of January

1709.

Katherine & Elenor ye twin daughters of Lewis Watkin baptis'd Oct 22°

1709-10.

Katherine ye daughter of Edward Morgan baptis'd Janry 11°.

1710

Anne ye daughter of Humphrey Wilkin baptis'd Aprill 14th.
John ye son of John William bapt July 23
Joan ye daughtr of Robt John bapt Novber 13°
Charles ye son of Richard Morgan bapt Mar. 3°

1711

Elizabeth ye daughtr of William Rosser was baptis'd March 25th
Anne ye daughter of William Thomas was baptis'd Decemb' 19.

1712

Katherine ye daughter of Morgan Christopher was baptis'd May ye 4th
Elizabeth ye daughter of Sr John Aubrey Bartt was baptis'd Septembr 13th.

1713

Mary ye daughter of James Portrey was baptis'd July 1st.
Eleanor ye daughter of Lewis Watkin was baptis'd Decemb' 14
Anne ye daughter of Robert John was baptis'd Janry 8

* Surname omitted query *Hugh*

1714.

Jane ye daughter of Mr Jno Edmonds was baptis'd Apl 20th

1715.

Mary ye daughter of Wm Miller was baptis'd July 6th
Thomas ye son of Mr Jn Edmunds was baptis'd March 11

1716

Mary ye daughter of Evan Rees was baptis'd Sept 12th
Anne ye daughter of Wm Miller was baptis d Decembr 21
Edward ye son of Edward Lewis was baptis'd March ye 18th
Frances ye daughtr of Sr Jn Aubrey Bart baptis d June 1

1717

Evan ye son of Robert John was baptis'd June 10th
Isaac ye son of Evan David bapt July 17th
William ye son of Saml William was baptis d July 30th
Sarah ye daughter of Lewis Watkin was baptis'd Sept 19th
Margarett ye daughtr of Sr Jn Aubrey Bartt baptis'd Octobr 25.

1718.

John ye son of Griffith was baptis'd March 26
John ye son of Mr John Edmunds was baptis'd Novembr 29th
Isaac ye son of Evan David was bapt Novembr 30th
Penelope ye daughter of Sr Jn Aubrey Bt bapd November the 18th
Lewis ye son of John Lewis was baptised Janry 11th
Margarett ye daughter of John Lewis was baptis d ye 27th of June 1722 [*sic*]

1719

John ye son of William Scipio was baptis'd Oct 31.

1720

John ye son of Jon Evan baptis'd Mar 25
Mary ye daughter of Rob John baptd Aug 25
Eleanor ye daughter of Evan David baptd Febr 12

1721.

William ye son of Wm Thomas bapd July 17.
John ye son of Wm Miller bapd Febry 11

1722.

William ye son of Edwd Lewis baptd Mar 27
Richard ye son of Tho David Sept. 13th

1723.

Thomas ye son of John David baptis'd Augst 16
Elizabeth ye daughtr of Evan Davd bapt Sept 5o
Anne ye daughter of Jn Miles bapt Sept 6o

1724

Winifred ye daught^r of Edwd Lewis baptis'd June 11th
John ye son of Jerdyn Bottyn baptis'd Septr 25th
Joan ye daughter of Wm Thomas baptis'd Oct 14th
Joan ye daughter of J^n William baptis d Decemb' 23th

1725

Thomas ye son of Edwd Watkin baptis d July 29th

1725-6

John ye son of Will. Thomas baptised March 17th

1726

Francis ye son of Evan David baptised April 12th
William ye son of Jerdyn Bottyn baptis d 8^{ber} ye 21
Edmund ye son of Mr Charles Davis Curat baptised x^{ber} ye 4

1726-7

Cissill ye daughter of John Lewis was baptised ye 19 of Febrewary
Lidia the daughter of Thomas David was baptised ye 22th of Febrewary

1727

Jane the daughter of Will Miller was baptised ye 31th of May
Watkine ye base sone of Christopher Morgan was baptised the 15th of 8^{ber}.
Mary the daughter of Edward Lewis was baptised ye 27th of 8^{ber}

1728.

Mary the daughter of William Thomas was baptised ye 1 of Aprill
Lidia the daughter of Lewis John was baptised March ye 29
John the sone of Cristopher Courtney was baptised ye 18 of Aprill

1728-9

Mary the daughter of Jenkin Dawkin was baptised March the 20th.

1729

David the sone of William Jenkin was baptised July the 30th
Catherin ye daughter of Edward Morgan was baptised August ye 20th
Charles the son of Mr Charles Dauis was baptised the 27th of Augst.
William the son of Euan Dauid was baptised the 19th of 9^{ber}.

1730

Thomas the sone of Morgan Euan was baptised the 10th of Aprill
Anne the daughter of Thomas Stradling was baptised Aprill ye 22th
Hanna the daughter of Reese Will' was baptised the 27 of May.
Euan the sone of Euan Dauid was baptised July ye 30th
Anne & Cessill ye twin daughters of John Lewis was baptised Augst the 19
Joan the daughter of William Thomas was baptised 8^{ber} the 15th
Joan the daughter of Evan William was baptised 8^{ber} the 21th
Edward the sone of Edward Morgan miller late desc^d was baptised 9^{ber} ye 18th

1730-1.

Mary the daughter of Lewis Howell was baptised Janewary the 1
William the sone of Jenkin Dowkim was baptised March the 24th

1731.

John the sone of George Lucras [*sic*] was baptised Aprill the 14th.
Anne the daughter of Euan Dauid was baptised Aprill the 15
Thomas son of Xtopher Courtney was baptized Apr. 18 being Easter Day.
Lidia the daughter of Lewis John was baptised June the 16th
Katherin the daughter of Euan William was baptised 8ber the 20th
William the sone of Mr Charles Dauis was baptised 9ber the 29

1732

Mary daughter of Jordan Boteing was baptized May ye 5th
William the sone of Reese William was baptised May ye 24th.
Richard the sone of Phillip Dauid was baptised the 7th of June.
Mary the daughter of William Jenkin was baptised the 15 of June
Elizabeth the daughter of Morgan Evan was baptised ye 21 of June
Richard and Katherin twins sone and daughter of Edward Lewis was baptised Augst ye 10th.
Anne the daughter of Cristopher Courtney was baptised 8ber ye 4

1732-3

Katherin the daughter of Euan Williams was baptised Janewary ye 15th.

1733.

Thomas the sone of Euan David was baptised the 9th of May

1733-4

Richard son of Edward Lewis was baptized ye 23th day of January
William the sone of Lewis John was baptised March ye 6

1734.

James the sone of Mr Charles Dauis was baptised Aprill the 19th
Joan the daughter of Reese William was baptised May the 29
Thomas the sone of William Jenkin was baptysed 9ber the 21
Joan ye daughter of Euan William was baptised xber the 16.

1734-5

Eleanor the daughter of Euan David was baptised Janewary the 9.
Thomas the sone of Christopher Morgan was baptised March the 14.
Courtney the sone of William Thomas was baptised March the 19th.

1735

Mary the daughter of Charles Morgan was baptised the 2 of Aprill
Anne the daughter of John How was baptised December the 28

1735-6

Euan the sone of Rees Williams was baptised Febrewary the 18th.

1736

Elizabeth the daughter of William Jenkin was baptised Mai 2
Mary the daughter of Morgan Morgan was baptised September 22[d]
Robert the son of Lewis Howell was baptised December 18
Christopher the son of Jenkin Dawkin was baptised December 30th.

1736-7

Mary the daughter of Christopher Morgan was babtised January 9th
Mary the daughter of Robert Cooke Rec[tr] of Lantrithyd was baptised February y[e] 6th
Margaret the daughter of Evan William was baptised March 4th 1736 [*sic*]

1737.

Constance the daughter of Thomas John was baptised Mai 5th.
Jane the daughter of Lewis John was baptis'd July 6th
John the son of John How was baptised November 23
Jane the daughter of Lewis Howell was baptis'd December the 16

1738.

William the son [of] William Lewelin of Leech Castle was baptised here July 5th
Jane the daughter of Edward Jenkin was baptised August 10
Priscilla the daughter of Christopher Morgan was baptised November 26

1739

William the son of Evan Williams was baptised June 7th
John the son of M[r] Thomas Edmonds was baptis'd July 25.
Cicil the daughter of Morgan Morgan was baptised September 29
Robert the son of Lewis Howell was baptised February 2[d]

1739-40

Anne the daughter of William Morgan was baptised March 3

1740

William the son of Jenkin Dawkin was baptised April 18.
Jane the daughter of Christopher Morgan was baptised Aprill 20
Eleanor the daughter of Lewis John was baptised Mai 3
Margaret the daughter of John How was baptised Mai 8
Jane the daughter of John Christopher was baptised August 16
Anne the daughter of David William was baptised September 7th

1742.

Thomas the son of M[r] Thomas Edmonds was baptised Oct[br] 22

1744

Frances y[e] daughter of M[r] Thomas Edmonds was privately baptiz d Nov[r] 10th, and received into y[e] Congregation Nov[r] 28th

1745

Margaret ye daughter of Thomas Evan was baptized Mar 31
Elizabeth ye daughter of Christopher Morgan was baptized August 30th
John ye son of David William was baptized Octr 13th
John ye son of David Cook was baptized Decr ye 4th.

1746.

Sarah daughter of Jacob Jenkin was baptized April 25th
John the son of John Christopher was baptized April 27th
Robert son of Leyson Thomas was baptized May 14th
Philip base son of Gwenllian was baptized May 25th.
Ann daughter of Lewis John was baptized July 20th
Mary daughter of Lewis Howell was baptized Decr 12th
Charles son of Lewelin David was baptiz'd Decr 17th

1747

Margaret daughter of Charles Matthew was baptized May 13
Mary daughter of John Christopher was baptized June 3d.
William son of Nehemiah Hopkins Rectr & Mary his wife was baptized Sepr 9th
Thomas the son of Thomas Evan was privately baptiz'd the 13th of Jany Admitted into the Congregation the 16th of Jany
Elizabeth daughter of David Cook was baptized February 5

1748

Alice daughter of Richard Gibbon was privly baptiz'd Ap 16. Recd into ye Congregn May 26
William son of Leyson Thomas was baptd June 9
Mary daur of Jacob Jenkin was bapd Sept 21

1749

Barbara daughter of Richard Gibbon was privately baptiz d Apl 23 Received into the Congregation May 24
Robert the son of Robert William was baptized July the 23d.
Edward the son of Thomas Evan the miller was baptized August 25th
Mary daughter of John How was privately baptized Sepr 15 Received into the Congregation Octr 5th
Margaret daughter of Lewis Howell was privately baptized January 13th Received into the Congregation February the 2d

1750

Gwenllian the daughter of Thomas Evan was baptized March ye 30th
Thomas the son of Nehemiah Hopkins Rector & Mary his wife was baptized April ye 2d
William son of Leyson Thomas was baptized Aprill 22d
Joan daughter of David Cook was baptiz d April 29th
Anne daughter of Richard Thomas was privately baptiz'd May 30th Received into the Congregation June the 20th
Margaret daughter of John Christopher and Jane his wife was baptiz'd March ye 20th

1751

Eleanor the daughter of Edward Lewis & Margaret his wife was baptized May 28th
Nehemiah the son of Nehemiah Hopkins Rectr and Mary his wife was baptiz d Augt 7th

Mary the daughter of Thomas Evan of the Mill was privately baptiz'd Augt 26
Elizabeth daughter of Edmund Davis was baptiz'd Augt 30
John the son of John Lewis was baptiz'd Sepr 18th
John the son of David Griffith was baptiz'd Sepr 20th

1752. New Stile.

Anne daughter of Lewis Howell was baptiz'd March 18th
Anthony son of Denham Jephson Esqr was privately baptiz'd May 23^d. Rec^d into the Congregation October 21
Mary daughter of Nehemiah Hopkins Rect^r & Mary his wife was privately baptiz d May 27
Jane the base-born daughter of Edward Matthew was privately baptiz'd Augt 17th. Received into ye Congregation Octr 11th
Evan the base-born son of Richd Rosser of Myrthyr Mawr was privately baptiz'd Augt 17
Gwenllian daughter of Thomas Evan of the Mill was baptized Octr 11
Jenkin the base-born son of Jenkin Owen was baptiz'd Octr 21
Mary daughter of Richard Thomas was privately baptiz d Octr 19.
Catherine the base-born daughter of John Crowley was privately baptiz'd Nov 23^d Rec^d into the Congregation Decr 7th

1753.

John the son of Denham Jephson Esqr was privately baptiz'd May 16 Received into the Congregation Feby 24 1754
William the son of Thomas Morgan was baptiz d May 14th
John the son of Edward Lewis was baptiz'd Octr 8th
Anne the daughter of Nehemiah Hopkins Rect^r was privately baptiz'd Octr 22^d
William the son of Richard Thomas was baptiz d Novr 25
William the son of Edmund Davies was privately baptiz'd Decr 20

1754.

Thomas the son of John Lewis was privately baptiz d May 6 Received into the Congregation May 31
Miles the base-born son of   was baptiz'd June 14
Anne the daughter of Leyson Thomas was baptiz'd Septemb^r 15th
John the son of Lewis Howell was baptiz'd Septemb^r 29th
Mary the daughter of Mr William Nichols of Camain was privately baptiz'd Novr 11th, and received into the Congregation Decr the 4th

1755

Jane the daughter of Thomas Evan of the Mill was privately baptiz d Decr 28, and received into the Congregation Jan^ry the 9th 1756

1756.

Margaret the daughter of Benjamin Griffith was baptiz'd Octr ye 10th

1757.

Mary Evan the daughter of Thomas Evan of the Mill was baptized January the 14th
John the son of Thomas Morgan was privately baptized March ye 23^d, and received into the Congregation ye 12th of April

1758.

Thomas the son of Thomas David Junr of Stonohad was baptized the 28th day of May

Mary the daughter of Thomas Morgan and Catherine his wife was baptized the 31st day of May

Mary the daughter of Leyson Thomas and Anne his wife was baptized the 2d day of June

Robert the son of Richard Thomas and Mary his wife was baptized the 19th of November

1759

William the son of Lewis Howel was baptized January 3d

Thomas the son of Watkin Rees was privately baptized January 22d, and received into the Congregation February 21st

Anne the daughter of Alexander Bevan was baptized the 18th day of February

Mary the daughter of Edward Mathew was privately baptiz'd Apl the 13th, and received into the Congregation May ye 9th

Elizabeth the daughter of Thomas Morgan cooper was privately baptized the 4th day of Decembr, and received into ye Congregation Decr the 14th

1760

Thomas the son of Thomas Morgan labourer was baptized February 20th

Robert the son of David Griffith was baptized May 9th

William the base-born son of William Fitz-Patrick & Elizabeth Jenkin was baptized May 27

1761

Catherine the daughter of Thomas Lewis was baptized May 22d

Cate the daughter of Leyson Thomas was baptized August 5th.

George the son of Alexander Bevan was baptized September 2d.

Mary the daughter of Richard Thomas was baptized Octobr 4th

Thomas the son of Lewis Howel was baptized December 4th

Edward the son of Edward Samuel was privately baptized Decr 14th

1762.

William the son of William Griffith was privately baptized May 6th, and received into the Congregation May 23d

Thomas the son of Thomas Richard was privately baptized June 9th, and received into the Congregation the 30th of June

David the son of Thomas Lewis was baptized June 16th

Elizabeth the daughter of Edward Mathew was baptized June 27th

John the son of Thomas Morgan labourer was baptized August 4th

Catherine the daughter of Thomas Morgan cooper was baptized September 8th

1763

Elizabeth the base-born daughter of Joan Lewis was baptized January 12th

William the son of William Dawkin was baptized March 30th

Mary the daughter of William Harry of the parish of Welch St Donats was baptized the 24th day of April

1764.

Winifred the daughter of Richard Lewis was baptized January 13th

Nicholas the son of William Morgan was baptized January 15th

Elizabeth the daughter of Alexander Bevan was baptized June 24th
John the son of Edward Jones was privately baptiz'd July 20th, and received into the Congregation July 25th
Thomas the son of John Lewis was privately baptized August 28th, and received into the Congregation September 26th
William the son of Thomas Richard was privately baptized Novembr 13th, and received into the Congregation the 7th day of Decembr
Christopher the son of William Dawkin was baptiz'd Novr 16

1765

Anne the base-born daughter of Lewis Howell the younger was baptiz'd Febry 2d
Christopher the son of Thomas Morgan labourer was privately baptiz'd March 1st, and received into the Congregation the 17th
Mary the daughter of William Griffith was privately baptiz'd May 11th, and received into the Congregation on the 19th
Elizabeth the daughter of William Jenkin was baptiz'd May 15th
Thomas the son of Thomas Lewis was baptiz'd May 22d
William the son of John How the younger was baptiz'd July 21st.

1766

Edward the son of Edward Jones was privately baptized February the 20th, and received into the Congregation the 19th day of March
Gwenllian the daughter of James Jones was baptized the 28th day of May
Mary the daughter of John Lewis was baptized the 2d day of July.
Catherine the daughter of Edward Matthew was privately baptized the 16th day of July, and received into the Congregation the 10th day of August

1767

Elizabeth the daughter of Francis Morris was baptized the 25th day of January.
Mary the daughter of William David was baptized May the 3d
Alexander the son of Alexander Bevan was privately baptized July 13th, and received into the Congregation the 2d day of August
William the son of Thomas Richard was baptized the 16th day of August
Jane the daughter of Lewis Howell was baptized the 27th day of September

1768

Jane the daughter of Thomas Lewis was baptized the 22d day of January
Elizabeth the daughter of Thomas Morgan of the Pentre was baptized the 10th day of April.
Edward the son of John Lewis was baptized the 22d day of June

1769.

Anne the daughter of William Jenkin was baptized the 11th day of January
Evan the base-born son of Evan Morgan labourer and Jane Bassett was privately baptiz'd June 20th, and received into the Congregation the 25 ditto
John the son of William Rees was baptiz'd June 28th

1770

Thomas the son of Lewis Howell and Sarah his wife was baptized March 7th
Margaret the daughter of Thomas Owen was baptized June 17th
David the son of Thomas Richard was baptized the first day of July

Catherine the base-born daughter of Evan Morgan and Jane Thomas was baptized August 29th
John the son of Thomas Morgan and Catherine his wife was privately baptized Sepr 10th, and received into the Congregation the 3d day of October
Anne the daughter of John Lewis and Mary his wife was baptized Sepr 28th
Thomas the son of Francis Morris and Mary his wife was baptized Novr 23d

1771.

Anne the daughter of William Thomas and Joan his wife was baptized February 3d
Mary the daughter of William Rees and Mary his wife was baptized February 8th
Elizabeth the daughter of William John and Anne his wife was baptized March the 27th
Margaret the daughter of William David and Catherine his wife was baptized April 7th
John the son of Thomas Lewis and Jane his wife was baptized April the 24th
Patty-Mary the daughter of Mr Mumford and Elizabeth his wife was baptized May 31st.
Margaret the daughter of William Jenkin and Rebecca his wife was baptized Novr 10th
Thomas the son of Thomas Owen and Mary his wife was baptized Decr 11th

1772

George the son of George Evan and Mary his wife was baptized May 20th
Catherine the daughter of Lewis Howell and Sarah his wife was baptized May 24th
Catherine the daughter of Edward Mathew and Elizabeth his wife was baptized July 1st
Elizabeth the daughter of John Hopkin and Barbara his wife was baptized August the 30th

1773

William the son of William John and Anne his wife was baptized February the 7th.
Anne the daughter of William David and Catherine his wife was baptized July 11th
Jenkin the son of Francis Morris and Mary his wife was baptized July 30th
Mary the daughter of Thomas Richard and Mary his wife was baptized August 1st
Henry the son of George Taylor collier was privately baptized September the 12th, and received into the Congregation the 26th
John the son of Thomas Owen and Mary his wife was baptized November the 21st

1774

Jane the daughter of William Jenkin and Rebecca his wife was baptized March the 23d
James the son of Lewis Howell and Sarah his wife was baptized June the 5th.
Catherine the daughter of Thomas Morgan and Catherine his wife was baptized June the 22d

1775

Anne the daughter of John Watson and Eleanor his wife was baptized March the 19th
David the base-born son of David Richard of Aburthin was baptized Apl 20th
Thomas the son of William John and Anne his wife was baptized the 14th day of May
Elizabeth the daughter of Lewellin Yorath and Jane his wife was baptized the 22d day of October
John the son of William David and Catherine his wife was baptized the 18th day of Novembr
Cecil the daughter of Edward Mathew and Elizabeth his wife was baptized Decembr 24

1776

Catherine the daughter of William Rees and Mary his wife was baptized the 8th day of May
Barbara the daughter of Thomas Lewis and Jane his wife was baptized the 30th day of May
David the son of John William and Anne his wife was baptized July 17th
Elias the son of Alexander Bevan and Mary his wife was privately baptized Sepr 28, and received into the Congregation Octr the 25th
William the son of William Jenkin and Rebecca his wife was baptized Octr 9th.

1777.

Edward the son of Thomas Rees and Catherine his wife was baptized May 4th
Mary the daughter of Mathew Hicks and Mary his wife was baptized May 9th
James the son of Thomas Morgan & Catherine his wife was baptised May 20th
John the son of Job David and Catherine his wife was baptized July 30th
Lyza Frances the daughter of Joseph Twycross and Hannah his wife was baptized November 9th
Rachel the daughter of John Lewis labourer was baptized Decr 6th
Elizabeth the daughter of Edward Bassett and Margaret his wife was baptized Decr the 19th

1778

Lidia the daughter of John Watson and Eleanor his wife was baptized July 19th
William the son of William Rees and Mary his wife was baptized Augt the 19th
Anne the daughter of William John and Anne his wife was privately baptized Sepr the 4th, and received into the Congregation the 27th of the same month
Edward the son of Job David and Catherine his wife was baptized Novr the 29th
Catherine the daughter of Edward Bassett and Margaret his wife was privately baptized Decr 7th, and received into the Congregation the 6th day of Jany 1779

1779.

Jennett the daughter of Mathew Hicks and Mary his wife was baptized February the 21st
John the son of Alexander Bevan and Mary his wife was baptized April the 14th.

1780.

Eleanor the daughter of John Lewis labourer and Joan his wife was baptized May 15th.
Mary the daughter of William John and Anne his wife was baptized Septr 10th.
William the son of Job David and Catherine his wife was baptized Octobr the 22d.

1781

Mary the daughter of Edward Bassett and Margaret his wife was baptized Febry 25th
James the son of Alexander Bevan and Mary his wife was baptized Septemr 21st
Margaret the daughter of William Rees and Mary his wife was baptized Octobr 18th
Catherine the daughter of John Lewis labourer and Joan his wife was baptized Decembr 6th

1782

Anne the daughter of Mathew Hicks and Mary his wife was baptized February the 2d
Mary the daughter of Edward Lewis and Elizabeth his wife was baptized April 28th

Mary the daughter of Thos Morgan and Jane his wife was baptized May 5th
Mary the daughter of Lewellin Yorath and Mary his wife was baptized October 13th
Elisabeth the daughter of Thos Thomas & Cathrine his wife was baptized the 10 of November
David the base-born son of Lewis Loyd was privately baptized the 3d of November, & received into the Congregation the 17th of the same month
Ann the daughter of William Humphry and Ann his wife was baptized December 25th.

1783

Jenkin son of Evan Jenkin & Jane his wife was baptized February 9th
Evan son of Job & Catherine David his wife was baptized March 16th
Thomas son of William Rees & Mary his wife was baptized August 24th.

Duty takes place

1784.

Thomas Digby son of Richard Aubrey Esqr was privately baptiz'd in the Parish of Lanblethian the 2d day of December 1782, and received into the Congregation in this Church the 3d of June 1784
Margaret daughter of Edward Bassett and Margaret his wife was priv baptiz'd 22d of June, and receiv d into the Congregation the 4th of July
John the son of John Lewis labourer and Joan his wife was baptized the 22nd of August

Examined & duty rece d by Edwd Lewis

1785.

Margaret the daughter of Matthew Hickes and Mary his wife was baptized March the 17th.
Ann the daughter of Thomas Jenkin and Kate his wife was baptized the 17th of April
Mary the daughter of John Watson and Elenor his wife was privately baptized the 23rd of April, and received into the Congregation the 5th day of May
Mary the daughter of Evan Jenkin and Mary his wife was baptized the 28th of April
William the son of Alexander Beavan and Mary his wife was baptized June the 12th
Mary the daughter of Thomas Thomas and Cathrine his wife was privately baptized June the 12th, and received into the Congregation the 3rd July

Examd & duty rece'd so far by Edwd Lewis

Margaret the base-born daughter of John Jones and Jane Jenkin was baptized the 25th of December

1786.

Barbara the base-born daughter of Thomas Lewis (son of John Lewis farmer) and Ann Thomas was baptized Jany 29th
Margaret the daughter of William Rees and Mary his wife was baptized 26 Febv

1787.

Thomas son of Thomas Jenkin and Kate his wife baptiz'd 20th May
William son of William Rees and Mary his wife was baptized August 5th
Barbara daughter of Thomas Thomas and Cathrine his wife was baptized October the 21

1788.

John the son of Mathew Hicks and Mary his wife was baptized January the 17
David the son of John Lewis and Joan his wife was privately baptized April the 18th, and received into the Congregation the 4 of May

Thomas the son of Thomas Lewis junior labourer and Ann his wife was baptiz'd June the 8.
Margaret daughter of Evan Perkins and Mary his wife was baptized November the 29

1789

Jane the base-born d[r] of John Watson was baptiz'd May 8th.
Samuel son of Thomas Lewis and Ann his wife was baptized August 8th.
Evan son of Matthew Hix and Mary his wife was baptized November 22nd

1790.

William son of John Williams and Allice his wife was baptized Jan[ry] 3rd
Elizabeth daughter of John Williams and Allice his wife was baptized January 3rd
Mary daughter of Tho[s] Jenkin and Catherine his wife was baptized April 3[d]
David son of David Lewis and Jennet his wife was baptized May 2nd
William the son of John Lewis and Joan his wife was baptized May 9th
John son of Tho[s] Thomas and Catherine his wife was baptized May 30th.
Dina daughter of John Howel and Margaret his wife was baptized June 6th
Elizabeth daughter of John Perkins and Elizabeth his wife was baptized July 16th
Bloom son of George Williams, Rector, by Sarah his wife was baptized the 22nd of September

1791.

Mary daughter of John Williams and Alice his wife was baptized the 27th of Feb[ry]
Mary dau[r] of David Lewis and Jennet his wife was baptized Dec[r] 25

1792 *

Eunice daught[r] of John Howell by Margaret his wife was baptized 13th May
David the son of Evan John by Elizabeth his wife was baptized 27th of May
Catherine daughter of Tho[s] Jenkin by Catherine his wife was baptized 29th of April
Maria daugh[r] of Morgan Aubry by Margaret his wife was baptized the 24th of June
William son of John Perkins Esq[r] by Elizabeth his wife was baptized the 5th of July
Margaret daught[r] of John Williams by Alice his wife was baptized 25th July
Elizabeth daught[r] of William Morgan by Catherine his wife was baptized 10th Oct[r].

1793.

MORGAN DAVID C. Warden.

George son of George Williams Rector by Sarah his wife was baptized the 27th of March
Edward son of John Perkins Esq[r] by Elizabeth his wife was baptized the 12th Dec[r]

1794

EVAN MEREDITH C Warden

Richard the son of Morgan Aubry by Margaret his wife was baptized the 12th of June
Thomas the son of David Lewis by Jennet his wife was baptized the 17th of August.
Julia Frances daugh[r] of George Williams, Rector, by Sarah his wife was baptized 13th Oct[r].
Margaret daught[r] of Thomas Jenkin by Catherine his wife was baptized 19th Oct[r]
Charlotte illegitimate daugh[r] of Edward Bird was baptized the 28th of Dec[r]

* From this date onward the Baptisms in the original are near the end of the book

1795

Thomas son of Thomas William by Ann his wife was baptized 15th March
Jehoiadah son of John Howel by Margarit his wife was baptized the 5th of April
William and Barbara the children of Robert Morgan by Mary his wife was baptized 29th of April

EVAN MEREDITH continued Churchwarden ever since the 14th inst April 1795

Cecil daughter of Evan Meredith by Elizabeth his wife was baptised 17th July
William Henry Cadogan Perkins was baptised the 20th Octr son of John Perkins by Elizabeth his wife
Philip son of George Williams, Rector of Lantrithyd, by Sarah his wife was baptised the 16th of December

1796

WILLIAM REES Churchwarden

Thomas son of Morgan Aubry by Margaret his wife was baptized the 5th of March
William son of William Morgan by Catherine his wife was baptized the 25th of Octr 1795 (*sic*)
Lewis son of William Aubry by Mary his wife was baptized the 24th of March
Thomas son of Thos Griffith by Jane his wife was baptized the 1st of May

1797

DAVID WILLIAM Churchwarden

John son of Morgan Aubry by Margaret his wife was baptized the 18th of Feby
Richard son of David Lewis by Jennet his wife was baptized 25th March
William son of Thomas Jenkin by Catherine his wife was baptized the 18th of June
Julia Frances the second daughtr of that name of Geo Williams Rector by Sarah his wife was baptized the 28th of July
Richard son of John Perkins by Elizabeth his wife was baptized 29th October.
Mary daughtr of William Aubry by Mary his wife was baptized 1st November

1798

EDWARD LEWIS Churchwarden

Richard son of Richard Watkin was baptized 25th March
Edward illegitimate son of Neddy Lewis by Mary of Pantmeyrick was baptized the 22nd of April
Thomas son of Thomas Evan by Ann his wife was baptized the 6th of May
Thomas son of George Williams Rector by Sarah his wife was baptized the 1st day of Septr
Harriet Maria daughter of John Perkins by Elizabeth his wife was baptized 18th Septr

1799

WILLIAM AUBREY Churchwarden

Mary daughr of Evan Meredith by Elizabeth his wife was baptized 23d Jany
Richard son of William Williams by Margaret his wife was baptized 22nd March
Leyson Thomas son of Thomas Jenkin by Catherine his wife was baptized 31st of March
Thomas son of Lewis David by Mary his wife was baptized the 26th of May
Thomas son of Thomas Evan by Ann his wife was baptized the 15th of June
Ann the daughter of Morgan Aubrey by Margaret his wife was baptized the 16th of June

Mary the daughter of William Aubry by Mary his wife was baptized the 21st of July
John son of John Watson by Mary his wife was baptized 3d Novr

1800.

THOMAS MORGAN Churchwarden

William son of Richard Watkin by Mary his wife was baptized the 16th of Feby
Owen Glendour son of George Williams Rector by Sarah his wife was baptized the 23d of February
Ann the daughter of John How by Ann his wife was baptized the 29th of March

1801

EDWARD LEWIS Churchwarden

Frances the daughter of George Williams Rector by Sarah his wife was baptized the 28th day of March
Catherine the daughter of Thomas Griffith by Catherine his wife was baptized the 3d of April
Thomas illegitimate son of William David was baptized the 24th of May
William son of David Lewis by Jennet his wife was baptized the 26th of July
Jane daughter of Thomas Evan by Ann his wife was baptized the 30th of Augt.

1802

EVAN MEREDITH Churchwarden

William son of Richard Meazy by Mary his wife was baptized 30th of May
Edward son of William David by Mary his wife was baptized the 15th of Augt
Thomas son of Evan Meredith by Elizabeth his wife was baptized the 19th of Decr

1803

THOMAS EVAN Churchwarden

Thomas son of Richard Watkin by Mary his wife was baptized the 17th of April
Catherine the illegitimate daughter of Daniel Lewis by Mary William spinster was baptized the 7th of August
Richard the illegitimate son of Richard Lewis by Ann John spinster was baptized the 4th of Septr
William son of Thomas Griffith by Catherine his wife was baptized 24th Novr

1804.

WILLIAM REES Churchwarden

Margaret daughter of Thomas Gibbon by Jane his wife was baptized 4th of March
Thomas son of Thomas Rosser by Catherine his wife was baptized the 3d of June
Elizabeth daught of Morgan Aubrey by Margaret his wife was baptized the 20th of June
Margaret daughr of Morgan Aubrey by Margaret his wife was baptized the 20th of June
William son of Thomas Evan by Ann his wife was baptized the 9th of July
Richard son of Richard Mumford by Catherine his wife was baptized the 18th of July
Ann the illegitimate daughter of Richard Lewis by Ann John spinster was baptized the 8th of Novr

1805

MORGAN AUBREY Churchwarden

Sarah daughter of Thomas Gibbon by Jane his wife was baptized the 20th of Jan^{y}
Thomas son of Thomas Williams by Jennet his wife was baptized 31st of March
Howel son of Howel Thomas by Eleanor his wife was baptized the 5th of July
Mary daugh^{r} of Richard Watkin by Mary his wife was baptized 28th July

1806.

SAMUEL WATERMAN Churchwarden

Ann daught^{r} of Thomas Griffith by Catherine his wife was baptized 1st of January
Æsop Charidemus the illegitimate son of Richard Lewis by Ann John spinster was baptized the 5th of January
Barbara daughter of Edward Thomas by Jennet his wife was baptized the 4th of February
Charles son of Thomas Gibbon by Jane his wife was baptized the 23^{d} of February
Barbara daughter of William Thomas by Barbara his wife was baptized the 28th of July
James Horatio son of William Vaughan Serjeant in the Royal Glamorgan Militia by Ann his wife was baptized at Bristol in the Messhouse on the 6th day of September 1806 by me George Williams Rector of this parish & Chaplain to the above Corps
Thomas son of Morgan Aubrey by Margaret his wife was baptized the 10th of Nov^{r}.

1807

CHRISTOPHER MORGAN Churchwarden.

Gwenllian daugh^{r} of Evan Harry by Margaret his wife was baptized the 4th of Jan^{y}
William illegitimate son of Richard Mumford by Mary Griffith spinster was baptized 4th of Jan^{y}
Margaret daugh^{r} of Christopher Morgan by Ann his wife was baptized 16th Feb^{y}.
Susanna daugh^{r} of Thomas William by Jennet his wife was baptized 22nd of March
Mary daughter of Edward Howell by Catherine his wife was baptized 2nd April
Jane daughter of Howell Thomas by Eleanor his wife was baptized the 3^{d} of May
Mary the base-born daughter of Thomas Harry of Bonvilstone was baptized the 3^{d} of May
Susanna daugh^{r} of Thomas Gibbon by Jane his wife was baptized the 25th of October.

1808.

RICHARD MUMFORD Churchwarden.

Jane daughter of Edward Thomas by Jennet his wife was baptized 15th Jan^{y}
Mary daughter of Thomas Evan by Ann his wife was baptized 15th June
Catherine the daughter of John Gwyn by Mary his wife was baptized Octr 16th.

1809

RICHARD MUMFORD continued Churchwarden

Thomas son of Thomas Richard by Catherine his wife was baptized 2nd of Feb^{y}
David son of William Thomas by Mary his wife was baptized 24th of May
John son of Richard Watkin by Mary his wife was baptized 25th of June
Elizabeth daughter of Richard Mumford by Barbara his wife was baptized 5th Nov^{r}

1810

RICHARD MUMFORD continued Churchwarden.

David son of Thomas William by Jennet his wife was baptized the 4th of February.
Ann daughter of Edward Thomas by Jennet his wife was baptized the 6th of Feby.
Harriet Sophia daughter of Morgan Aubrey by Margaret his wife was baptized the 3d of June
David son of David Jenkin by Lydia his wife was baptized the 16th of Septr
John son of John Gwyn by Mary his wife was baptized the 4th of Novr

---

MEMORANDA

Memorandu' that the xxvth daye of June 1637 Annoq' R Rs D'ni n'ri Caroli &c tercio decimo Sr Thomas Awbrey of Lantrithed in this Countie of Glam'gan Knight out of his Christian and Charitable disposic'on and entent that the releeff of the poore of the said p'ishe may be augmented hath wth his owne handes the day afforesaid given and deliu'ed to the handes of Will'm John and Morgan John Churchwardens and Rice Howard and Mathew ffrancis ouerseers of the poore of the said p'ish for this p'sent yeare the some of Tenn Powndes of good and lawfull money of England vpon truste Confidence and Condic'on that they the said Churchwardens and ouerseers of the poore and their successors shall yearly dispose of the said tenn powndes according to their discrec'on wth the approbac'on and Consent of Edward Pricharde Batchelor of dyvynity now incumbent of the rectorie of the said p'ish and his successors to the best advantage. And shall bestowe and dispose the yearly benefitt p'fitt and encrease yssuing from the said some to and amongst the poore of the said p'ishe against eu'y the ffeastes of the nativitie of our Lorde and Easter yearly for their better releeffe Provyded alwayes that the said tenn powndes shall remayne be resrved & Continue as a stock for the said purpose wthin the said p'ishe.

THO AWBREY

Teste
EDW PRICHARD
HENRY FFORNYSS.
ANTHONY MEYRICKE

RICE HOWARD
WILLIAM JOHN
MORGAN JOHN
MATHEW FFRAUNCES

Memorandu' also that the said daye the said S[r] Thomas Awbrey out of his Charitable disposic'on hath given bestowed and wth his owne handes deliu ed to William John and Morgan John Churchwardens of the said p'ishe of Lantiethed for this p'sent yeare to the vse and for the benefitt of the Churche ther (and to remayne and to be vsed as a Com'union Cupp) one silver standing Cupp gilt wth a Cover annswerable thervnto The same cupp to remayne and be pres'ved as the rest of the Churche goodes there by the Churchwardens afforesaid and their Successors for the purpose afforesaid, provided that yt shalbe lawfull for the Churchwardens for the tyme being wth the assent & direcc'ons of the incumbent of the rectorie there to change the forme and fashion of the said Cupp & Cover as occasion shall require so that noe p'te of the value therof be diminished.

Tho: Aubrey

Teste
Edw Prichard
Rice Howard
Henry ffornyss

William John, } g ard
Morgan John, }

BURIALS.

The names of them that be buried wthin the p'ish of Lantrithed as foloweth

1571.

Elizabeth Mathew buried A Thursday the xvth of Februarij
Rice Haward buried A Thursday the viijth of Marche.
Dauid ab John buried A Tuesday the third of Aprill
Evan Elice buried A ffriday the xjth of August.
Richard Morgon buried the second of November

1572.

John Willia' sonn to W^{m} D'd buried A Monday the xiiijth of Aprill.
Agnes Haward buried A Saterday the xiijth of September
Jonne servant to Mr Mancell buried the viijth of March.

1573

Willia' Mancell sonn to Mr Mancell buried A Twisday the xxvjth of May.
Edward sonn to Mr Mancell buried A Saterday the viijth of August

1574.

Alson Fabian buried A Monday the iiijth of Januarij
Janne Gwin buried A Wensday the xth of November
Joann Richard daughter to Thomas Richard buried A Sonday the xiiijth of November
Morgan dio (?) Piere buried A Monday the last of December

1575.

Jonne Gwin buried A Monday the third of Januarij
Willia' Hugh buried A Thursday the vjth of Januarij
Wenllia' Gitto (?) buried A Saterday the xxijth of Januarij
Willia' Howell buried a Thursday the xvijth of Februarij
Joann Howell buried Twisday the vjth of December.

1576

John Dauid buried a Twisday the xiiijth of February.

1577.

George ap Morgan buried a Saterday the xjth of May
Agnes Rice buried A Twisday the xth of September
Katerin Jevon buried A Thursday the xxth of Marche

1578.

Agnes daughter to Jenkin Dawkin buried A Saterday the xxjth of June
Jenett daughter to Griffith Willia' buried A Monday the third of Nove'ber
Alexander Chalk sonn to Willia' Chalk buried A Twisday the xxvth of Nove b'
Elizabeth daughter to Robert Deere buried A Saterday the xiiijth of Dece ber

1579

Morgan Willm buried A Monday the xxiijth of ffebruarij
Margery Willia' buried A Wensday the xjth of Marche
John Gwin buried A Wensday the vijth of October

1580

Elizabeth wif to John Web buried A Thursday the xxijth of Januarij
John sonn to Thomas Raglon buried A Sonnday the xxjth of Februarij
Thomas W^{m} servant to Mr Mancell buried A Twisday the xxvijth of September
Morgan ap Willia' buried A Thursday the vjth of December

1581

Joann Whitney wif to John Mancell buried A Sonnday the vijth of Januarij
Ric sonn to John George buried A Thursday the viijth of June
John ap Pric buried A ffriday the viijth of September
Jenkin sonn to David Jenkin buried Mvnday the xxvth of September

1582.

Margarett Willia' buried A Twisday the xvjth of Januarij.
Adam Hugh buried A Mvnday the xxvjth of Februarij

1583.

Margarett Johns servant to Mr Mancell buried A Sonnday the xiijth of January
Jevonn Gisonn buried A Saterday the xth of Marche
Wenllia' Adam buried A Thursday the xxjth of Marche
John Richard buried A Saterdaye the xxth of July
Miles sonn to Mr Rimbror Mathewe buried A Mvnday the second of Septe'ber
Katerin wiff to John Richard buried A Sonnday the xxixth of Septe'ber
Rice sonn to Mr Anthoin Mancell buried A Mvnday the xviijth of November

1584

Elizebeth wif to John Thomas buried A Thursday the xxvijth of Februarij
John David buried the second of August
Morice Goch buried the xxviijth of November

1585

John Willia' Bassett buried the xth day of Januarij

1586, 1587

[*No entries*]

1588

Johan Steephen buried A ffriday the xviijth of Maij
Blanch Awbre daughter to Mr Thomas Awbre buried A Mvnday the second of Dece'ber
David sonn to Rice Chalk buried A Twisday the third of Dece'ber.
Elizabeth David buried A Sonday the viijth of December
Elizabeth doughter to Rober ap Price buried A Sonnday the xxixth of December

1589

Jevon ap Prichard buried A Sonday the xxvjth of Januarij
Edward sonn to John Willia' buried A Mvnday the third of Februarij
Joann Jevon servant to Mr Mancell buried A Mvnday the xxvjth of Junij
John Edward and Jonett Fleming buried A Thursday the xxvjth [*sic*] of March

1590

Mary Jupp (?) buried A Saterday the xxvth of Julij
Joann Donni (?) buried A Sonday the xxijth of November
Mary Turbill buried A Twisday the first of December

1591

Margarett Jevon buried A Sonday the vijth of Februarij
Joann Steephen buried A Mvndav the xxvjth of July
Cissill Awbre daughter to Mr Thomas Awbre buried A Mvnday the 23th of August
Mary daughter to Mirick ap Jevan buried A Wensday the xxijth of Dece'ber

1592

Morgon Jevon buried A Wensday the vth of Januarij
Cissill Haward daughter to Willia' Haward buried A Twisday ye xxvth of Januarij.
Jenett wif to Thomas Richard buried A Thursday the xxiijth of March
Wenllian doughter to John Deere buried A Sonnday the xxvjth of March
Matho Taylor buried A Thursdaye the xjth of Maij
Rice Howell buried A Mvnday the xixth of June
Christian Dio buried A Thursday the xxth of Julij
Richard sonn to Thomas Richard buried A Thursday ye xiiijth of September.
John William buried A Friday the xiijth of October
Jennett Mathewe wif to Willia' Haward buried A Wensday the xviijth of October
Matho sonn to David Dawkin buried A Mvnday the xiiijth of Dece'ber

1593

Willia' Bassett buried A Friday the second of Marche
Howell Willt buried A Twisday the xvijth of Aprill
Mallt Morgan buried A Wensday the xvjth of Maij
Hugh sonn to John Willia' buried A Mvnday the xxvth of June
John Bassett of ye Game buried A Thursday the vjth of September
Georg sonn to Jenkin Mathew buried A Wensday the xxvjth of Dece'ber.

1594

Johan wif to John Willia' buried A Saterday the xijth of Januarij
Mary wif to Ric Howell buried A Twisday the xxixth of Januarij
Morgon Jevon sonn to Jevon Thomas buried A Mvnday the xxvth of Februarij
John Rosser buried A Twisday the xxjth of Maij
Wilsiford daughter to Mr Thomas Awbre buried A Twisday the second of Julij
Jevon ap Price buried A Mvnday the xvjth of December

1595.

Anne Richard buried A Sonnday the second of Marche
ffraunces Harry sonn to Richard Harry buried A Mvnday the xxjth of Aprill
John Bassett buried A Wensday the xxiijth of Aprill
Maud Willia' wif to Lewis David buried A Wensday the iijth of Dece'ber
Jenett wif to John Mathew buried A Twisday the xxiijth of March

1596.

Willsiford doughter to Mr Thomas Awbre buried A Thursday the xxixth of Aprill.
Elizabeth daughter to James Bassett buried A Saterday the xijth of June
Robert Deer buried A Friday the xijth of September
Willia sonn to Richard ap Price buried A Sonnday ye xix of September
John sonn to David Dawkin buried A Friday the vth of November
David ap Jevon *alias* Mayson buried A Mvnday the vjth of Dece'ber
James sonn to Richard Harry buried A Sonnday the xiith of December
James sonn to Dauid Willia buried A Mvnday the xiijth of December

1597

Mary wife to Thomas Bassett of ye Garne buried A Sonnday the seco'd of Januarij
Caterin daughter to Thomas Richard buried A Friday the vijth of January
ffraunces sonn to D d Willia' buried A Twiesday the first of Februarij
Wenllia daughter to D d Dawkin buried A Wensday the vjth of Aprill
Agnes wife to John Morgon buried A Twisday the xixth of Aprill
Cissill doughter to Richard ap Price buried A Twisday the xxvjth of Aprill
John Web buried A Mvnday the ixth of Maij
Wenllian Elice buried A Sonday the vijth of Auguste
John Elic buried A Sonndaye the xxviijth of Auguste
Wenllia' Richard buried A Wensday the vijth of September
Willia' Deere buried A Mvnday the xijth of December

1598

Margarett Thomas buried A Wensday the viijth of Februarij
Jenett doughter to John Mathew buried A Twiesday the xiiijth of Februarij
Margery doughter to John Willia' buried A ffriday the xvijth of Februarij
Mary doughter to D d Dawkin buried A Saterday the xviijth of Februarij
John Dio buried A ffriday the third of Marche
Joann Adam wif to D'd Dawkin (or Dowkin) buried A Saterday the xvth of Aprill
Anne Tyrheirne* buried A Thursday the viijth of June
Anthonie sonn to Richard Harry buried A Wensday the xiiijth of June

1599.

Margarett Morgan buried A Thursday viz the iij of Maij
David Thomas buried A Saterday viz the xvjth of June
John sonn to Griffith Howell buried A Saterday viz the xxijth of Dece ber
Dame Elizab Wallwin wife to Richard Wallwin Knight was buried the 10th of Februarij

1600.

Mansell Aubrey ye son of Tho Aubrey Esq was buried ye 28th day of July.
Willia' Basset ye son of Tho Basset was buried ye 29th day of July
Myricke Griffith miller was buried ye 22th of Dece b
Jane Rosser the daughter of John Rosser was buried the 13^{tth} of March

1601.

John Daukin the son of D d Daukin was buried the first of April A o p'dict
John Daukin the son of D d Daukin was buried the 2° of April's An o p dict
Willia' ffrancis the son of Mathew ffrancis was buried the 22th die August
Marsly Thomas the base daughter of Joan Deare was buried the 27th die Nove b' An o p'd ct

* *Query* Ircherne?

1602

Rice Evan the son of Evan Thomas was buried the first day of June An'o p'dicto
Mary Dawkin the daughter of David Dawkin was buried the six and twentith day of August
Catherin Dew the daughter of John Dew was buried the seaven and twentith day of December
Thomas Williams was buried the twentith of March
Barnaby East borne w^tin the cou'tie of Surrey returninge from Ireland (where he served his ma^tie as a souldier) homeward, died in the p ishe of Lantrytheed and was buried 23th of March

1603

Elizabeth Williams widdow was buried 28th Julj
Phillip Earle was buried 22th of August
Cissill Myricke the daughter of Myricke Evan of Leech Castell was buried the third day of November
Myricke Yeavan of Leechcastell was buried the 14th of Januarj.

1604.

Robert ap Prece was buried the 20 of April
Katherin Richard vidua was buried the 13th of Julj
Jane Basset the daughter of James Basset was buried the 11th of Novemb
Anthonie Mansell Esqr was buried the 13th of Novemb'

1605

Elizabeth Yevan the daughter of Roger Yevan was buried the 27th of April
Alis Dew the daughter of John Dew was buried the 6th day of June
Margret Mathew the daughter of John Mathew taylor was buried the 18th of June
William Haward was buried the 28th of Novemb'
Richard Thomas the son of Richard Tho de Lechcastell was buried the 1° of Febr

1606.

Anthony Mathew the son of Morgan Mathew was buried the 16 day of May
Hugh ffrancis the son of Math ffrancis was buried 17 die Junij
Anthony Dawkin the son of D d Dawkin was buried the 25 of Julij
Blanch Basset the daughter of James Basset was buried 23 Januarij

1607

Catherin the daughter of Mathew Rosser was buried 11° of Aprilis
David the son of Tho Dawkin was buried 29th Aprilis
John son to Anthony Gwin Esqr was buried the 29th Maij
Gillian Edw the wife of John Edw. was buried the 12th of Julij
Elizab Mansell widdow was buried the 24th of Dece'b'
W^m the son of Morgan Haward was buried the 25 of ffebruarie

1608

Eliza Gwyn the wiffe of Wm Penry was buried the 10 day of Aprill
Eliza the daughter of Wm Penry was buried 17° Aprilis
Elizab the daughter of Tho Dawkin was buried 31 of July

1609

An' the wife of Jenkin Matho was buried 2do die Marcij

1610

Thomas John was buried ye 13th of May

1611

Cissill the daughter of Wm Thomas was buried 2do Marcij
Hughe Robbet was buried 29 of Dece'b
Joan Basset the daughter of Thomas Basset was buried Januarij

1612

Gwe llian Thomas was buried 30 Aprilis
Wm Bersey was buried 9° Maij
James David the son of David Wm was buried 7° Maij
Mary George was buried 10 die Maij
Elizab Richard widdow was buried 3d die Julij
John Mathew taylor was buried 24 die Dece'bris
Anne a Price was buried the 26 die Dece'bris

1613.

Thomas Johns the father in law of James Bassett was buried the 25 of April
Thomas Bassett was buried 2do Augustij
An' Bisset the wiffe of John George was buried 17 of Septemb
Catherin Dawkin was buried [*no date*]
Thomas Gwyn the son of Mr Anthony Gwyn Esqr [*sic*] was buried 21 Marcij

1615

Anthony Gwyn the son of Mr Anthony Gwyn Esqr [*sic*] was buried 25 of May
Mathew Rosser was buried 6° August
Anthony the son of Edward Jenkin was buried 17° Januarij
Johannes Hicks ludimr sepultus erat 1° die Marcij

1616.

Thomas the son of David Jenkin Esqr was buried 2° Maij
An' the daughter of Rich Harry was buried 7° Maij
Cissill the daughter of Rich Thomas de Leichcastel buried 3° Decemb
Tho Bassett de Garne was buried 9° Februarij

1617

Lewis Dawkin was buried 22° Aprilis
Wm Gwyn' the son of Mr Anthony Gwyn was buried 4° Maij
Mary the daughter of Mr Robert Buttun was buried 17° Maij
Alice the daughter of Edward Prichard was buried 6° day Junij
ffrauncis Cadocke* was buried 17° die Junij
Mary the daughter of Mr David Jenkins was buried 18° Junij

1618

Katherin Adam widdow was buried 11° Aprilis
Ginnett the daughter of Tho Younge was buried 24 Aprilis

* *Query* Cradocke.

William Edward was buried 14° Januarij [*sic*]
Lewis Phillip was buried 23 Junij
Thomas Aubrey the son of Sr Edward Aubrey Knight of Brecon was buried 12 of Januarij

1619

An' Penry vidua was buried 7° die Augustij
Richard Haukins was buried the eleventh day of Septemb'
Gynnett Thomas was buried the 16 of Februarij

1620

Gwenllian the daughter of Wm Morgan was buried 31° Maij
Margrett Morga' was buried 31 Julij.

1621

Anthonye the son of Richard Adam was buried 4° Aprilis
Jenkin Mathew was buried one Thursday xxvj° die Julij
Agnes Mason vid was buried one Wensday xij° Novembris

1622

Lewis the son of David Jenkins Esq was buried 6° Aprilis
Elizab David was buried 23° Aprilis
Katherin Thomas wass buried 13° Maij
Alis Evan the wiffe of Mathew ffrancis was buried 28° Maij
Anne ye wiffe of Rich Adam buried 3° July
Christian ye daughter of Edward Jenkin was buried Novemb'
Arnold Bassett was buried ij Januarij
Magdalena filia Edwardi Prichard, rect^r^, erat sepulta 11° ffebru
Anna Jones vxor Ricei Haward erat sepulta 17° ffebru

1623.

Jane W^m^ vidua was buried 10 die Aprilis
An' the daughter of David Jenkins Esq was buried 14 Aprilis
Barbara Basset the daughter of James Basset was buried 21° Maij
William Thomas was buried the 19° of Julij
James Bassett was buried the 19° of Julij
Mary Jones was buried the 6° of August
Alis Morgan was buried the 13th of Novemb
Anthony Penry was buried the 19th of March.

1624.

David ye son of Wm Hullin was buried 20 die Octob
Elizab the daughter of Thomas Jenkin was buried 30 die Augustij
John Hugh was buried 10 ffebru
Elnor the wiffe of William Edward was buried 12 Marcij

1625.

Katherin Lewis was buried decimo nono die Sept

1626

William Morgan was buried decimo nono die Junij
Cissill Dawkin was buried Augustj

1627

Mary Nicholl the wiffe of Thomas Deere was buried sexto Aprilis
Isabella the servant of Widdow Bassett was buried 18° Junij
Katherin Jones the wiffe of Morgan Haward was buried 2° Augustij

1629

William Haward was buried 3° of Maij
William Penry was buried 19° of Junij
Mary Dawkin of Tregousse was buried 25° of June
Mary Harry was buried 24° Augustij

1630

Roger ap reece was buried decimo Julij.
Thomas Powell was buried xjth day of Febru
Richard Harrie was buried the on and twentith day of ffebruarie

1631.

John Jen^a^n of the Greene Way was buried 23° Aprilis.
Jane Dawkin was buried 9° Octob
Marie Matho the wiffe of Edward Eles of Tregouse was buried the third of Septemb'
Margrett Cooke the wiffe of Jenkin Cooke of Boulston deceased was buried 9° die Novemb'
Ann Bassett the wiffe of Richard Harrie was buried 8° Decemb

1632

Jen^a^n Thomas was buried decimo die Aprilis
Ann the daughter of Rice Wilkin was buried the xxth of May.
Margrett Hullin the wiffe of Wm Matho was buried the three and twentith of May
Eva Robin was buried the seaventh of Julij

1633

Ann the wife of Roger Lewis was buried 30 Decemb
ffriswith Morgan was buried 10 ffebru.

1634

Mary the daughter of Mathew ffrancis was buried 12° May.
Robert the son of Edward William of Burthin was buried 29 Julij
John the weaver was buried the 21 of Decemb'
Cissill Thomas was buried the 23 of Decemb'

1635

Wenllian Howel was buried 27 Marcij
Cissill the daughter of Wm John was buried 22° 8bris
Dame Marie Awbrey was buried the tenth day of November

1636

Katharina filia Roberti Thomas erat sepulta 4° Augustj
Edwardus Jenkin sepultus erat 22° Augustj
Edwardus Sobe sepultus erat 3° 9bris
Thomas Deere sepultus erat 28° 9bris
Myricke Roger was buried 12 Dece'b'
Godwinus Prichard, Vicarius de S[t] Mary Hill juxta Gelligarre,* sepultus erat 24 Dece b
Richard ap Jen[a]n was buried 9[no] Jan'rij
Katherin W[m] the wiffe of George Dawkin was buried xj[mo] Aprilis
Thomas Hopkin was buried 19° Marcij

1637

Elizabetha filia Johannis Awbrey Arm' sepeliebatur tricessimo primo August'

1638.

Ciselia filia Johan'is Awbrey sepeliebatur decimo nono Sept'b'
Joanna Deere sepultus [*sic*] erat 10 Jann'
Elizab the wiffe of Morgan Price was buried xxx[the] of Jann'
Nest John the wiffe of William Edward was buried 5° ffebr.
Eduardus Prichard S T B huius Eccl'iæ Rector sepultus fuit 5to Martij

1639.

ffranciscus Rosser filius Mariæ Jo[n] vid. sepultus fuit 22° Apr.

1641

Sr Thomas Awbrey Knight was buried the two and twentith daie of November

1642.

Elenor the wiff of Thomas Awbrey Chauncelor of St Dauies was buried Aprill 24.
Elizabeth Griffith the wiff of John Euan of ffewlace in the p'ish of Lancaruan was buried in Lantrithed the xxvj[th] of August

1643—1647.

[*No entries*]

1648.

William Jones was buried the second of November.

1649

John Harry was buried the second day of December
M[r] Laomedon ffowler Rector of Lantrithyd was buried the seaventeenth day of Aprill

1651

Philemon Prichard was buried y[e] 4th day of November.

1653.

Tanglwyst Jones buried 29th of June
Lettice Howard buried 5[t] of Septemb

* Gellygaer, co Glamorgan?

1654.

William Mathewe buried 24th of Decemb

1655.

Anthony Jones buried Aprill 4th

1658.

Katherin the wife of James Bassett was buryed the xxijth of December

1659

Morgan Howard was buryed the xvth of January

1660

Rice Howard was buryed the 25th day of October

1664.

John Howard the sonne of Rice Howard was buried 21th of Aprill
John Howard of the Close was buried the 5th of May
John the sonne of John Dyer was buried 28th day of May
Elizabeth Prichard late wife of Mr Edward Prichard, Batchelor of Diuinity, late Rector of this church, was buried the 22th day of June
Cisell Penry the wife of Harry Roberts was buried the first day of July.
Cisell the daughter of Thomas Powell was buried the 20th day of Auguste

1665.

Ivon ffrancis was buried the tenthe day of June
John the sonne of Anthony Rosser was buried the 9th day of Auguste
Gorge Jenkin of this parish was buried the 17th day of November
John the sonne of Thomas Powell of Tregoosse was buried the 24th day of December
Mary the wife of Roberte Dauid was buried the 4th day of January.

1666

Margarette Rees widowe was buried the 16th day of July
Susan Bassette was buried the 12th day Auguste
Anne the wife of Richard Bassette of the Garne was buried the 19th day of September
Margarette Lewis the wife of Anthony James was buried the 9th day of January

1667.

Mary the daughter of Thomas Powell was buried the 22th day of October

1668.

Margarette William the daughter of Anne William widow was buried the 2th day of Auguste
ffriswith Arnold widow of the parish of Welsh St Donats was buried the 3 day of September

1669.

Elizabeth the daughter of Anne Leonard of this parish was buried the 4th day of July
Anthony Rosser of this parish was buried the 30th of September
Elizabeth the wife of Anthony Roberte of this parish was buried the first day of November
Elizabeth the daughter of Richard Bassette of the Garne was buried the first day of January
Gwillim David was buried the 9th day of March
John Bassette of the Crosse was buried the 17th day of March

1670.

Thomas Leonard of this parish was buried the 3 day of May
John the sonne of William John of this parish was buried the 9th day of May.
Amy the daughter of Dauid Thomas of Llanguion was buried the tenth day of June
Jenette the wife of Jenkin Johne of this parish was buried the seventh day of Auguste
Watkin Dauid of this parish was buried the 16th day of Auguste
Elizabeth the wif of X'pher Rosser of this parish was buried ye .
Flourens Evan widdow of Coychurch was buried here ye . .
Anne Rosser widdow of this p ish was buried ye
Anne George widdow of this p'ish was buried ye
Elizabeth ye wife of Tho Howell of this p ish was buried ye . . .
Jenkin Williams, Mr of Arts & Rector of Llantrithid, was buried the seuenteenth day of December
Margery Phillip widd of this p'ish was buried the 18th of December
Mary the wife of John Jay of this parish was buried ye 2d of ffebruary
Nest . was buried the servant of Sissill Edward of this p'ish the 18th of ffebruary
Will the son of Will Jon of this p'ish was buried ye 27th of ffebr
Edward Rosser of this p'ish was buried the 21th day of March

1671.

Wenllian the wife of John Reece of this p'ish was buried the 27th of March
Jenkin John of this p'ish was buried the thirtieth day of March
Mathew David of Welsh St Donatts was buried in this church 13th of Aprill
ffrancis Kendell of ye p'ish of Welsh St Donatts was buried in this church ye 8th of May
Tho Howell of this p'ish was buried ye 10th day of May
Evan David of this p'ish was buried ye 16th day of August
Owen Morgan of this p'ish was buried ye 18th day of August
Anne ye wife of Phe Rob't of this p'ish was buried ye first 7ber

1672.

John Jay of this p'rish was buried the 13 of May

1673.

Sicill the daughter of Benjamin Langton of this p'rish was buried the second day of June
Thomas Awbrey, Bachelor of the Laws and Chancellor of the Diocess of St Davies, of the p rish of Bolwinston was buried in this church the 20th day of November
Scicill the wife of Anthony Howard was buried the ninth day of December.
Ann the daughter of William John of this p rish was buried the 16 of January
William Rosser the sonn of Edward Rosser was buried the 8th day of ffebruary
Margaret Dawkin the daughter of Jenkin Dawkin was the same day and year [*sic*]

1675

Edward Lloyd was buried the 26 day of October
Mary Menicks the wife of Gwillim David was buried the 29th of October
Lydia Mathews the daughter of George Mathews of Barry was buried the 1 day of November
Mary Thomas the wife of Robert Thomas was buried the 1 day of November 1671 [*sic*]
Katherin Edward the wife of Will John of the Green Way was buried in August 1674 [*sic*]
Elizabeth Turbervill the wife of David Turbervill was buried the 22th of October 1674 [*sic*]
Alse Turbervill the daughter of David Turbervill & Elizabeth his wife was buried 1675

1676, 1677

[*No entries*]

1678

Jane John wife of Thomas Rosser was buried ye 17th of 9ber

1679.

Sr John Awbrey Knt & Bart was burried ye 9th of January
William ye son of Anthony Howard burried 10ber the 28
Tho ye son of Peter Leonard was burried the first of Jan'y
Margaret ye daughter of William Morgan of Landaffe burried 9ber 4th
John ye son of John Reece was burried 10ber the sixth
Lettice the daughter of Charles Howard was burried Feb ye 2d
Eliz Mathew ye base daughter of Mr Miles Mathew of Lankaioch was burried Feb ye 14th
Catherine Hugh ye wife of David Hugh was buried ye 24th of December.
Mary Euan ye daughter of Euan Dauid was burried ye 20th of March

1680

Mariæ Awbrey Conjunx Johannis Awbrey Equits et Barron' sepulta erat vicessimo quinto Martij
Cicilia George de Lantrithyd sepulta erat decimo sexto Aprillis
Mary John ye wife of John Christopher was buried ye 3d day of May
Anne John of Peterston e was buried in this p'ish church ye 28 of June
Mary the wife of Edward Rosser of this p'ish was buried January 24th
Jane the wife of Rees Morgan of this p'ish was buried ye 29 of January
John Bassett of this p'ish was buried March ye 23, de Garn.

1681

Joan John ye wife of Edward James of this parish was buried the 15 of August

1683

Joan ye daughter to John Christopher was buried ye 13 of Janvary.
Joan Reece the daughter of Reece Morgan ws buried the 28 of Janvary

1684

Edmundus Waters Lantrithyd Rector et vicessimo Martij nono vitam cum morte commutavit ac ejusdem ultimo die sepultus

Jacobus Wittney sepultus fuit octo deci'o Junij
Henry John was buried ye 16 of Octob
Henry Peirce was buried the 11 of Octo
Jane Adam was buried ye 15 of December.
Mary ye wife of John Bassett was buried ye 23 of December

1685.

Cicill the daughter of John Rees was buryed May the 8th
Mary ye daughter of Samuel Coale was buryed May 11th
William Dawkin was buryed July 15

1686.

Phillip Tracy was buryed September ye 27
David Thomas was buryed October ye 27
Miles ye son of Christopher Dawkin was buryed November 1st
Gwirrill David was buryed November ye 7th
Jane ye daughter of David Harry of St Mary Hill & Lydia his wife was buryed November 9
John ye son of Mr William Bassett of Garn was buryed December ye 22
Robert David was buryed January ye 10th.

1687

Hopkin ye son of William Hopkin was buryed Aprill 15
Thomas ye son of William John was buryed ye 15 of May being Whitsunday
Katherin Rees ye widow of Anthony Robert was buryed the 4th of June
Mr William Howard was buryed June 10
Samuell the son of Samuel Cole was buryed the 30th day of December
 the daughter of John Christopher was buryed the third day of January
Maud . was buryed Febr 28
John the son of Samuell Cole was buryed the 7th of March.

1688

Ann Watkin was buryed Aprill 25
Catherin the daughter of William Hopkin was buryed ye first day of December.
John Deane was buryed January 15th

1689

Christopher Scipio was buryed May 27
Ann Howard was buryed June 7
 the son of John Christopher was buryed Aug 9
Mathew ye son of Watkin David was buryed Aug 14
Margaret Morgan was buryed ye 10th of November
Morgan David ye son of Isaac David was buryed ye first day of January
Catherin Dawkin was buryed Jan 23^d
Mr St John Jones dyed in this parish Jan 26, & was buryed at Penmark Jan 30th.
Richard Scipio was buryed Jan 31
Mr William Basset of Garn was buryed March 16.

1690

Jenkin the son of Christopher Dawkin was buryed July 7th.
William ye son of Watkin David was buryed Nov 30th.

Jennet ye daughter of Watkin David was buryed Dec 6th
Mrs Elizabeth Jones of this parish was buryed att Penmark the 11th of December
Mrs Wenllian Howard was buryed the ninth day of January

1691

Elizabeth Llewelin the wife of Lewis Grono was buryed on May day.
Jane Robert ye wife of John Robert of this parish was buryed ye 19th day of June
Joan Deane was buryed Oct 22
Harry Robert was buryed Dec 31

1692

Ellenor the daughter of John Christor was buryed ye 10th day of September
Hopkin Jenkin was buryed Sept 13th
John Morgan was buryed Oct 2
Elizabeth ye wife of John David smith was buryed Jan. 28.

1693

Jane ye wife of Benjamin Launton was buryed Aug 29
Jennett Dawkin was buryed Dec 17
Mary Mathew was buryed Jan 14

1694.

James Hugh was buryed Aprill 1.
Stephen Rees was buryed May 10
Elizabeth Hopkin ye wife of Anthony Rees was buryed June 12
Jenkin Dawkin was buryed June 14
Joan ye daughter of Anthony Rees was buryed June 14
Elizabeth Mathew widdow was buryed Jan 16

1695

John David smith was buryed March 28th
Robert ye son of Reece Nicholes was buryed Apr 16th
Mary ye base daughter of Mary Lewis of ye parish of Loncarvan was buryed November ye 9th
Ann ye wife of Rice Morgan was buryed March 17th

1696.

Rice Morgan was buryed June 11th
Mrs Ann Gamage was buryed July 14th
Jennet ye wife of John Christopher was buryed Aug. 15
Margaret John brewmaid at Lantrithid was buryed Sept 27
George Rosser was buryed December 24th
Jane ye wife of Watkin David was buryed Decemb 29th
Margery ye daughter of William John was buryed January 10th
John ye son of Joan Dyer widdow was buryed Feb 6th

1697

William John ye son of William John Rees & Alice his wife was buryed May 31

1698

Jennett ye daughter of Llewelin Thomas & Alice his wife of ye parish of Dyvynnock in Brecknockshire was buryed Oct 5

Susanna ye daughter of Thomas Jenkin of Leech Castle & Ann his wife was buryed Oct 12
Charles Morgan a cooper by trade of this parish was buryed ye 11th day of January
George Rosser ye son of Elizabeth Rosser a poor woman on ye parish was buryed ye 12th of January

1699.

Thomas David was buryed the 3rd of September
Morgan William was buried the 20th of 10ber
John the son of John Courtney a poor man was buryed the same day

1700.

William John was buried the 12th of January
. the son of Nicholas Wilkins was buried the 21 of January.
Anne John of this parish was buryed the 2th of Febr
Samuel Cole was buryed the 18 of Febr
John Courtney was buryed the 30th of March
Margarett the wife of Tho Howell was buried the 10th of May
John the son of William Thomas was buried the 20th of July
Sr John Awbrey Barrtt was buried the 3 of 8ber
Elizabeth the daughter of Christopher Daukin was buried the 12th of 8ber
David the son of Watkin David was buried the 3 of December
Mary the daughter of William Watkin was buried the 20th of 10ber.

1700-1

Chatherine [*sic*] David was buried the 31 of January
Elizabeth Morgan was buried the 2d of February

1701

James Bassett was buried the 17th of June
Jane Mathew was buried the 12 of August
A beggar boy was buried the 27th of 7ber.
Philip Robert was buried the 28 of 9ber

1701-2

John the son of Gwilime Hugh was buried the 15 of Feb
Jane the daughter of William Thomas was buried the 20th of Feb

1702.

Jennet Howard was buried the 26 of Apr
David Turbervile of the Green-way was buried the 3d of July.
Jane the daughter of Anthony William was buried the 25th of August
Anne the daughter of Edward Morgan of Burthin was buried the 28 of September
Edward James was buried the 6th of October.

1702-3.

William John was buried the 26th of Feb

1703-4

Thomas Leweline gardiner was buried the 13th of March

1704

Isaac David was buried the 13th of Aprill
Anne the wife of Peter Leonard was buried the 5th of 9^{ber}
Anthony the son of Anthony William was buried the 8th of 9^{ber}.
Jane Kent was buried the 27th of Feb.

1704-5.

Mary the daughter of Tho Roberts was buried the 16 of March

1705

Mr Jenkin Leyster was buried the 9th of June.
Anne Leonard was buried the 16th of July
Christopher Anthony was buried the 23 of October

1705-6.

William Thomas of Leech Castle was buried the 1st of January
Mary Jenkin was buried the 2^{d} of Jan
John the son of Evan Morgan was buried the 21 of Jan.

1707-8.

Anthony Morgan was buried the 25 of Jan
Alic Griffith was buried the 30th of Jan
the son of William Thomas was buried the 18th of Feb.
William Morgan was buried the 24th of Feb
Anne Harry was buried the 27th of Feb
Thomas Rosser was buried the 2^{d} of March
Joan Dawkin was buried the 7th of March
Richard the son of Richard John was buried the 7th of March
Edward Powell, $Rect^{r}$ of Lantrythid, was buried March 14th

1708

Robert the son of Robert Howell was buried the first of Aprill
Benjamin Lancton was buried May 4°
Richard William buried May 18°
Thomas Roberts buried May 21°
Margarett Lewis was buried May 25
Lewelin Morgan buried May 27
Lewis y^{e} son of Lewis Howell was buryed Sept 4
Mary y^{e} daughter of $Rich^{d}$ Morgan buried Sept 6
Gwenllian David buried Sept 9
William Courtney buried Oct 26
Gwillim Hugh buried Nov 1st
Ailice Bassett Nov 8
Joan Dyer the wife of John Christopher buried Jan 28th.
Joan William buried March 4th
Elizabeth Roberts buried March 20.

1709.

Thomas Roberts buried March 25
Elizabeth ye daughter of Tho Roberts Mar 28

John Courtney buried July 11
Katherine ye wife of John Courtney buried July 12
Elizabeth ye daughter of Gwillim Hugh was buried Octob 29th
Elisabeth ye daughter of Isaac David buried Feb 5th

1710-11.

Thomas ye son of Anthony William buried Jany 30th

1711

Tabitha ye daughter of Anthony Morgan was buried Aprill 22

1712.

Edward Morgan was buried Oct. 21.
Margarett ye daughter of Sr John Aubrey Bartt was buried Novemb 3

1713

Edward Courtney was buried Apll 24
Jane ye wife of John Wilkin buried July 28o
Roderick William buried Nov 2o.
Marjery Morgan buried Dec 20
Francis Robert buried Dec 28.

1714

Maria uxor Johannis Aubrey Bartt sepulta fuit 7o die Julij
John Robert, Clerk to 5 Incumbents of this parish, was buried July 23
James Edward was buried Augst 2
Joan Rees widdow to Edward Watkin was buried Novber 29
Bridgett ye wife of Robt Howell was buried March 8th

1715

Robert William was buried Nov 5
Peter Leonard buried Jan 6
Anne Dawkin buried Jan 11

1716

Elizabeth Morgan buried June 5o
Elizabeth ye wife of Henry Richard was buried January 16
John Christopher was buried Febr 12o

1718.

William Hopkin buried May 7th
Thomas ye son of Robt Howell buried July 20.
Elizabeth Morgan widdow buried July 26th
Penelope ye daugr of Sr Jn Aubrey Bart was buried ye 20th of 9r.

1719.

Anne Hugh p was buried Oct. 17.
Cecil John buried Feb 24th

1720

Eleanor ye wife of Mr Jn Edmunds buried Mar 27

Cecil ye daughter of Tho Jenkin buried Apl 11.
Elizabeth Hugh p buried Augst 30
Thomas Jenkin p buried Decemb 19th
Elizabeth ye widdow of Gwilim Hugh buried Dec. 23.

1721.

William ye son of Christr Dawkin was buried Sept 25
Susan ye wife of Phil David burd Mar 23

1722.

Anne Dean p. was buried March 4th

1723

Philemon Morgan p buried Sept 6th.

1724

Samuel William p was buried July 9th
William ye son of Wm Hopkins Rectr of this parish was buried Oct. 31th.
Elizabeth Leyson widdow was buried Janry ye 13th

1725.

Jane Christophr spinster was buried Augst 26.

1725-6

Jane ye only daughter of Mr John Edmunds February 11th

1726

William Hopkins Rectr of this parish was buried April 22
Rees Sippio was buried Augst ye 9th
Margaret Morgan widdow was buried 8ber ye 22th
Lidia John widdow was buried 9ber ye 25

1726-7

Thomas Morgan of ye parish of Lancarvan was buried Janeway ye 27
Christopher Dawkin was buried Febreway ye 6.

1727

John William was buried 7ber ye 26
Mary Dean widdow was buried 8ber ye 8
William Sippio was buried xber ye 26th

1727-8

Lidia the daughter of Thomas David was buried Febreway the 10th
Anne ye wife of Lewis Howell was buried Febreway the 21th
Mary William p was buried Febreway ye 27th

1728.

Joan James widdow was buried March ye 28
Lettice William widdow was buried March ye 29
Edward son of Edward Morgan miller was buried May ye 14th.
Eleanor the daughter of Euan Dauid was buried July 11th
William Thomas was buried Agust ye 13
Anne Water was buried Agust ye 14.
Anthony William gardner was buried 7^{ber} ye 1.
Elizabeth the wife of William Watkin was buried 7^{ber} ye 5

1728-9.

Joan Morgan widdow of ye parish of Lancaruan was buried ye 9th of Janewary.
Thomas Dauid was buried Febrewary ye 11th
Cissill the daughter of John Lewis was buried Febrewary ye 19th
Margaret the wife of Thomas Rosser smith was buried March the 19th.

1729

Mary the daughter of Jenkin Dawkin was buried Aprill the 3.
Mary the daughter of Gorge Lewis of ye parish of Landaff was buried hear Aprill ye 21th
William Watkin was buried ye 24th of Aprill
Joan William widdow was buried ye 25th of May
Barbara the wife of Euan Dauid was buried July ye 10th
Lidia ye daughter of Lewis John was buried July ye 23th
Mrs Jennet Aubrey widdow was buried 8^{ber} ye 13
Joan the daughter of William Miller was buried 9^{ber} ye 30th

1729-30

William the son of Euan Dauid was buried Janewary the 1
Llewelin William was buried March ye 1

1730.

Catherin Dauid widdow was buried May ye 13.
Mary the wife of William Miller was buried May ye 16.
Anne the wife of Phillip Dauid was buried May ye 27
Lewis Watkin was buried July the 17th.
Samuell the son of Samuel Hughs of the parish of Philly was buried Augst the 27th
Joan the daughter of Euan Williams gardiner was buried 9^{ber} the 9th.
Mary the wife of John Lewis was buried 9^{ber} ye 25
Joan Lanclet widdow was buried x^{ber} ye 21th

1730-1

Hendry Richard of ye parish of St Hillery was buried here Febrewary the 26

1731.

William Miller was buried ye 22th of Apr
Mary Morgan of Tregoffe was buried May 2
Thomas son of Xtopher Courtney was buried May 9th
Thomas Thomas was buried June ye 1
William the sone of Jenkin Dawkin was buried June the 3
Catherin the daughter of Euan William was buried 9^{ber} the 2

1732

Cissill ye daughter of John Lewis was buried May ye 22th.
Jenet the wife of Euan Dauid was buried Aug^st^ ye 10th
Richard the sone of Edward Lewis was buried Aug^st^ the 12
Katherin the daughter of Edward Lewis was buried Aug^st^ the 13
Mr William Turberuill of ye Green way was buried 8^ber^ ye 30

1733

Margarett David was buried Aprill 22
Katherin Morgan widd was buried May ye 2
Mary Butler of Byrthin was buried Octr 11.
Ann Willott was buried Octr 29

1733-4

Joan Jenkin was buried Jan^r^ 12
Thomas the sone of Euan Dauid was buried Febrewary ye 27.

1734

Cissill Rosser was buried the 13 of May
Margaret Phillip of the parish of Lancaruan was buried August ye 13
Mrs Powell widd was buried 8^ber^ the 4
Mary the wife of James Dauid was buried 9^ber^ the 12
Thomas the sone of William Jenkin was buried 9^ber^ the 25

1734-5.

Mrs Courtney widd. was buried Janewary the 13th
Daniel John was buried the 7 of March

1735

Catherine Samuell of Bonvilston was buried ye 8th day of Aprill
Courtney the sone of William Thomas was buried July the 14.
Joan the daughter of William Thomas was buried Aug^st^ ye 5.
. . the base sone of James David was buried 7^ber^ the 22

1735-6

Rees Morgan of the towne of Cowbridg was buried hear the 8 of Febrewary

1736.

Robert the son of Lewis Howell was buried December 19

1737.

William Wilkin was buried April 16
James David was buried July 30th
William John of Penmark but born in this parish was buried August 16.
Thomas Rosser was buried September 26
Catherine the daughter of Morgan Christopher was buried November 16

1737-8

Evan Reese of the parish of Lanishen was buried March 12

1738.

William John of Carmain (?) was buried March 27
Charles Morgan was buried April 12
Elizabeth Thomas was buried April 26
Jane Howell was buried March 19

1739.

Bridget the daughter of Lewis Howell was buried March 28
Mary the daughter of Charles Morgan was buried March 29
Philip David was buried April 7th
William the son of Evan Williams was buried June 19
Henry Philip buried February 4th.

1740.

Jane the daughter of John Christopher was buried August 18

1741—1743.

[*No entries.*]

1744.

John ye son of Charles Matthews was buried Novr 23d.
Mr William Thomas was buried Feby 2d
James the son of Evan John was buried Feby 11th.
Robert ye son of Leyson Thomas was buried Feby 18th

1745.

Christopher the son of Jenkin Dawkin was buried April ye 3d.
Anne the wife of N Hopkins Rector of this parish was buried Sepr 18th.

1746

Mary daughter of Evan John was buried May 8th
Cecil the daughter of Morgan Evan was buried May 22d.
John son of John Christopher was buried June 7th
John Watkin was buried Feby 14th.

1747

Edward Morgan was buried July 24th.
Margaret daughter of Charles Matthew was buried Octr 27
William son of N Hopkins Rector was buried Decr 7th.
Anne base-born dar of Gwenllian bury'd Feb 28 [*sic*].

1748

Charles son of Cradoc Evan was bury'd Ap 12
Margaret wife of Morgan Christopher May 14.
Jacob Jenkin was bury'd July 12
Margaret base-born daur of Gwenllian bury'd Oct 31 [*sic*].
Morgan Christopher was buried Decr 26th.

1749.

Anne daughter of Thos Charles of Landaff was buried the 11th of May.
Mr Gronnow was buried October 11th

1750

Morris Thomas was buried Decr 4th
William Evan was buried Jany 25th
Evan William was buried Jany 27th

1751

Mary daughter of Thomas Evan of ye Mill was buried Augt 27

1752. New Stile

Mary wife of Henry John was buried Jan^{r} 24
Nehemiah son of N Hopkins Rector was buried February 22.
Mary daughter of N Hopkins Rec^{r} was buried May 30
Mary daughter of Nicholas Thomas was buried Octr 21
Jenkin base-born son of Jenkin Owen was buried Octr 25
Evan base-born son of Richard Rosser of Myrthyr Mawr was buried Aug^{t} [*sic*] 26
Elizabeth Matthew was buried Novr 25
Jane base-born daughter of Edward Matthew was buried Decr 7

1753

Barbara Miller was buried January 7th
Anne Hopkins widdow was buried April 30
Evan David was buried July 5
Anne the daughter of Nehemiah Hopkins Rect^{r} was buried Octr 25.
Mary the daughter of Sarah Jenkin widdow was buried Novr 25
Mary the wife of Edmund Davies was buried Decr 20

1754.

William the son of Edmund Davies was buried Jany 6th.
John Christopher was buried Octob^{r} 19th

1755

Edward the son of Thomas Evan of the Mill was buried February the 12th
Henry John was buried Novr 1st.

1756

Jane the daughter of Thomas Evan of the Mill was buried January 16th.
Winifred Lewis of this parish was buried May 28th

1757

Elizabeth the wife of John Hicks was buried Sepr 1st

1758.

Joan the wife of Thomas Morgan of Treguff was buried April 16.

1759.

Elizabeth the wife of Mr John Edmondes was buried the 10th day of January.
Mary the wife of Robert John was buried the 24th day of February
John Thomas of Cowbridge was buried the 29th day of October
Mary the daughter of Leyson William was buried the 1st day of December

1760

Mary Lavo was buried January 12th
Robert John was buried Febry 11th
Richard Thomas weaver was buried March 1st.
Winifred the daughter of Sarah Jenkin widow was buried April 25th
Hester the wife of Thomas Miles of Pistle Hill was buried Octr 20th

1761

Jennett the wife of John Lewis was buried May 6th
Margaret Dawkin widow was buried Decr 11th

1762.

Richard Thomas was buried March 26th
Edmund Davies was buried April 13th
Edward Lewis the elder was buried Sepr 24th

1763

Anne the wife of Benjamin Wilkin was buried May 30th

1764.

Lydia Dawson was buried July 30th
Thomas Watkin was buried Septembr 2d
Thomas Miles of Lancarvan was buried Septembr 7th.
Sarah the wife of James John was buried Octobr 6th

1765.

Gwenllian daughter of Thomas Evan of the Mill was buried the 31st day of March
William the son of Thomas Richard was buried the 10th day of May
Jane Christopher widow was buried the 29th day of August
Jennett Watkin widow was buried the 21st day of October.
John March was buried the 24th day of Novr

1766

Anne the wife of Edward Thomas of Treguff was buried the 1st day of April.
John of Leigh-castle was buried the 19th day of May
William FitzPatrick was buried the 21st day of May
Edward Jones was buried the 5th day of June.
Thomas the son of Thomas Evan thatcher was buried September 22d.
Elizabeth the wife of Thomas Evan thatcher was buried September 28th
Mary the wife of John William was buried Octr 20th
Henry Thomas of this parish was buried Octr 27th

1767

Edward Lewis was buried the 28th day of January
Anne Jenkin was buried February 14th
Edward the son of Edward Jones was buried February 24th
Margaret Jenkin was buried April 3d
Elizabeth Nicholas was buried April 21
Mary Evan was buried the 1st of May
Isaac David was buried the 3d of May
Sr John Aubrey Barontt was buried the 20th day of October
John Lewis was buried Decr 19th

1768

Margaret Lewis widow was buried March 27th
Margaret the wife of Benjamin Lee was buried April 14th
Thomas Cook was buried April 16th
Christopher Morgan of Leigh-castle was buried May 29th
Mary the daughter of Mary Thomas widow was buried Octobr 18th.

1769

Richard Robert of Leigh-castle was buried March 31st
John the son of Thomas Morgan farmer was buried July 11th
Catherine the daughter of Edward Mathew was buried July 13th.
Elizabeth Jenkin widow was buried Novr 13th
Margaret Lewis widow was buried Decr 11th.

1770.

John David was buried March 14th
John William was buried June 26th
Alice Morgan widow of Bolston was buried August 20th.
Mary the wife of N Hopkins Rector of this parish was buried Septr 18th
Eleanor the daughter of Margt Lewis widow was buried Sepr 24th

1771.

Catherine Dawkin was buried May the 30th
Catherine Robert widow was buried June 8th
Thomas Morgan of Treguff was buried Octobr 7th

1772.

Mary the daughter of Thomas Evan carpenter was buried May 16th
Mary the wife of David Griffith was buried July 18th

1773

Anne the wife of John Robert blacksmith was buried January 28th
Jennett the wife of Richard Lewis of Lancarvan was buried June the 4th
Jennett the wife of Thomas David was buried Novr the 15th.

1774.

Rachel the wife of Alexander Bevan was buried May the 13th
Mathew Thomas was buried Sepr 19th.

1775

Catherine the daughter of Thomas Morgan farmer was buried Apl 14th.
Thomas Owen labourer was buried June 18th
Lyson Thomas labourer was buried Augt 12th.
Mrs Jephson was buried Augt 22d
Mary the daughter of Joan William was burd Sepr 2d
Mary the wife of Mathew Hicks was buried Decr 2d
James John gardiner was buried Decembr 25th

1776.

Margaret the wife of John Robert was buried Janu^{ry} 1st
Anne the wife of Cradock Evan was buried February 6th
Mary March widow was buried October 6th

1777

John Robert was buried Janu^{ry} 5th.
Morgan Morgan was buried May 7th
Rachel the daughter of John Lewis labourer was buried Decr the 16th

1778.

John the son of Thomas Morgan farmer was buried the 14th day of June.
James the son of Thomas Morgan farmer was buried the 28th day of June
Anne Lewis widow was buried July 23^{d}
Edward the son of Mary Owen widow was buried Augt 28
Catherine the base-born daughter of Evan Morgan was buried Augt 29

1779

Margaret Lewis widow was buried Jany 16th
Rebecca the wife of William Jenkin was buried the 17th day of February.

1780

Cecil Hugh widow was buried April 22^{d}.
Thomas David miller was buried August 18th.
Thomas Morgan cooper was buried Novr 3^{d}.
Jane the wife of Lewis John was buried Novr 16th.

1781

Margaret Robert was buried Feby 3^{d}.
Lewis Rees was buried March 31st.
Maria Martha the daughter of Richard Aubrey Esqr was buried Octob^{r} 27th.

1782.

Alice Lewis spinster was buried March 2^{d}
John the son of John Lewis was buried March 6th.
Mary Lewis spinster was buried March 8th
William David was buried March 12th
Elizabeth Mathew widow was buried Mar 30th
Mary the wife of John Lewis was buried April 16
John Robert smith was buried May 19th
Barbara Charles was buried May 19
Margaret the daughter of William Rees was buried June 16
Gwenllian Robert was buried the 3^{d} of July
Elizabeth the daughter of William John was buried the 5th of July
Mary the daughter of William John was buried the 21st day of July
Mary Howell widow was buried the 23^{d} of July
Frances the wife of Richard Aubrey Esqr was buried the 20th of December

1783.

Margaret David of Lanmals was buried May 31.
Craddock Evan was buried June 22

Sarah the wife of George David of the parish of Lancarvon was buried September 21st
Duty takes place
Margaret Thomas a pauper of this parish was buried the 4th day of December.

1784.

Ann the wife of William Humphreys of the parish of Bonvilstone was buried November the 4th
Exd & duty rece'd by Edwd Lewis

1785.

William the son of William Rees was buried the 28th day of May
Elizabeth the wife of Richard Robert was buried August 18th
Exd & duty rece d so far by Edwd Lewis
Benjamin Wilkin was buried October 19th

1786

Edward Basset a pauper of this parish was buried June 14th
William Fitzpatrick a pauper of the town of Cowbridge was buried June 15th.
Sir Thomas Aubrey Baronet was buried the 13th of September
David the son of Thomas Richard was buried the 21st of Octbr

1787.

Elizabeth the wife of Lewis Howell was buried the 12th of June
Eleanor the wife of John Watson was buried November the 11

1788.

Mary the wife of Thomas Richard was buried the 26 of July
Mary Lewis spinster was buried the 24th of Septbr
Lady Aubrey widow of Sir Thomas Aubrey Baronet was buried the 14th of Decbr

1789

Rees the base-born son of Rees Morgan was buried the 20th of February
Edward Samuel of the parish of Penmark was buried the 18th of September
John the son of Alexander Bevan (pauper) was buried the 14th of November
Thomas Evan (carpenter) was buried the 16th of November

1790.

Thomas base son of Thomas Morgan was buried February 7th
Nehemiah Hopkins clerk was buried March 30th Rector of Lantrithyd
Matthew Hicks was buried the 6th of July
Robert Thomas was buried the 27th of July
Job David was buried the 7th of August.

1791

William Humphreys (an infant) was buried the 11th of March
Catherine David was buried the 20th of Sepber
Ann Thomas was buried the 21st of Octr.

1792

Joan Morgan was buried Aprill 13th

Watkin Rees was buried the 24th of May Paupr.
George the son of George Williams Rector of this parish was buried August the 2, by me W Thomas Curate of Cowbridge
Margaret daughr of John Williams was buried the 18th of August
Alice Williams was buried the 17th of Septr

Settled so far.

Ann William (a pauper) was buried the 16th of October
Lewis John was buried 29th Decr.

1793

MORGAN DAVID Churchwarden.

William Perkins was buried the 8th of Jany
Margaret Aubrey sister of the late Sir Thomas & daughter of Sir John Aubrey Bart was buried 22nd of Feby
Mary Mumford was buried 26th August

Settled so far

Cate Cristor was buried 27th Novr.
Mary Thomas was buried 6th Decr

1794

EVAN MEREDITH Churchwarden

John Lewis was buried 8th June

Settled the duty

1795.

EVAN MEREDITH continued Churchwarden

1796.

WILLIAM REES Churchwarden

Thomas Aubrey was buried 8th March
Alexander Bevan was buried 15th of April.
Julia the daughter of George Williams Rector of this parish was buried May the 27th, by me Richard Williams Curate of Lantrithyd
Elizabeth Jenkin was buried 27th May.
John Jones was buried 16th of October
Catherine Bassette was buried 13th of December.
George Evan was buried 19th Decemr.

1797

DAVID WILLIAM Churchwarden.

Margaret Evan was buried 29th Jany
Margaret Griffith was buried 1st of May
William Lewis was buried 6th Novr
Mary Aubrey was buried 9th Novr.
Richard Perkins was buried 19th Novr
Edward Matthew was buried 22nd May [*sic*]

1798

EDWARD LEWIS Churchwarden.

Catherine Lewis was buried 6th May

Thomas Evan (an infant) was buried 12th May
Thomas Robert (blacksmith & pauper) was buried the 15th of June

1799

WILLIAM AUBREY Churchwarden

Evan Hicks was buried 2nd Feby
Elizabeth Bassette was buried 17th April
Dina Howel was buried the 22nd of May

1800

THOMAS MORGAN Churchwarden

William Morgan (an infant who was killed by a bullock) was buried the 14 of January

1801.

EDWARD LEWIS Churchwarden.

Mary Meredith (an infant) was buried the 13th of January
Lewis Howel was buried the 21st Feby
Margaret Griffith was buried the 2nd of April
Margaret Rees was buried the 9th of June
Ann Thomas was buried 7th December

1802.

EVAN MEREDITH Churchwarden

Cecil Robert was buried 1st Jany
Elizabeth Daniel was buried 2nd Jany

1803

THOMAS EVAN Churchwarden

Thomas Thomas was buried 27th Janur
Mrs Jones was buried the 13th of Feby
Frances Williams was buried the 12th March.
Mr Mumford was buried the 22nd March
William Williams (an infant) was buried the 28th March
Ann Morgan was buried the 29th of March
Mrs Mumford was buried the 30th of March
Mary Thomas was buried the 10th of April
Richard Lewis (an infant) was buried the 16th of Septr
Mary William was buried the 25th Octr
Catherine Lewis (an infant) was buried 27th Oct
Thomas Lewis was buried 14th Novr

1804

WILLIAM REES Churchwarden

Elizabeth Thomas was buried the 31st of March
Thomas David (an infant) was buried the 29th of Septr
Ann Lewis (an infant) was buried the 14th Novr

1805.

MORGAN AUBREY Churchwarden

David Griffith was buried the 8th of Feby
William Rees was buried the 4th of August.

1806

SAMUEL WATERMAN Churchwarden

Edward Samuel (an infant) was buried 3d Feby
Jane Wilkin was buried the 24th of Feby
Æsop Charidemus Lewis was buried the 24th of Feby
Edward Lewis (aged 95) was buried the 15th of March
Ann Williams (an infant) was buried the 7th April
Thomas Richard was buried the 8th of April
Catherine Mumford was buried the 18 h April
Catherine Morgan was buried the 6th July
Ann John (who was accidentally shot at Lwynrithyd) was buried the 14th of July
Elizabeth Thomas was buried 11th August.
Ann David (widow) was buried 21st Octr

1807.

CHRISTOPHER MORGAN Churchwarden

Deborah Ellen Perkins was buried 25th Septr
William Griffith was buried 2nd Octr
John Day (an infant) was buried 12th Octr.

1808.

RICHARD MUMFORD Churchwarden

Jane Bevan was buried 16th Feby
Elizabeth Matthew was buried 21st Feby
Colonel Richard Aubrey was buried the 9th of April

1809

RICHARD MUMFORD continued Churchwarden

William Lewis was buried the 27th of July.

1810

RICHARD MUMFORD continued Churchwarden

Marianne Perkins was buried the 14th of January.
Thomas William was buried the 6th of May
Thomas Samuel (an infant) was buried the 25th of June
Ann Day (an infant) was buried the 27th of June

MARRIAGES.

The names of such as be maried wthin the p'ish of Lantrithed as foloweth

1571.

Jevon ab Jevon and Cissill Howell maried the xxiiijth of February
John ab John W^{m} and Mary John maryed A Sonnday the xjth of May
Estone ab Jevon and Jonne George maryed the xviijth of June

1572, 1573.

[*No entries*]

1574.

John Richard and Katerin John maryed A Saterday the vjth of Februarij
Jenkin Dawkin and Mary George maryed A Sonnday the second of Maij
Thomas ap John & Elizabeth Jones maried ye Saterday the xiijth of June
Willia' Nichol and Mary Richard maried A Sonnday the iiijth of Julij
David ab Jevon alias Mayson and Anne vz Thomas maried A Saterday the xvjth of October
Howell Peere and Jenett John maried A Sonnday the xxiiijth of November.

1575

[*No entries*]

1576

Lle'n Lewis and Joan Myrick maried A Wensday the last of February
John ap Morgan and Anne Willia' maried A Sonday the xiiijth of June
John Haward and Elizabeth Givon maried A Mvnday the xxth of August
Thomas Richard and Elizabeth Bassett maried A Sonndaye the xxvjth of August.
Rice Howell ( ) and Marye Matho maried A Mvnday the xxvjth of November

1577

John Gwin and Elizabeth Richard maried A Mvnday the xxixth of Aprill
Willia' Saphine and Katerin Fleming maried A Wensday the last of October
Willia' David and Cissill John maried A Saterday the xxith of October.
Christopher Portre and Johan Georg maried A Twisday the vth of November
Morice Mathew and Elizabeth Mathew maried a Thirsday the xxvth of Dece'ber

1578.

Richard Nicholas and Katerin W^{m} maried A Sonnday the viijth of June
Jenkin ap John and Malt Richard maried A Mvnday the xiiijth of Julij
Adam Hugh and Katerin Philipp maried A Twisday the xxj of October

1579.

Thomas David and Agnes George maried a Twisday the xiiijth of Januarij
John Somsonn [? Samsonn] and Wenllia' David maried A Saterday the ixth of Maij
David Jeritt and Alse Young maried A Thursday the xxjth of Maij
Jenkin ap Jevon and Elizabeth Thomas maried A Sonnday the xxijth of Nove'ber
John Thomas and Elizabeth John maried A Sonnday the xxixth of Nove'ber

1580

Thomas Pranch (?) and Jonne Mathew maried A Saterday the xxiijth of June

1581

[*No entries*]

1582

Jenkin Jevon and Mary Bassett maried A Sonnday the third of February

1583

[*No entries*]

1584.

Alexander H . . and Anne Strawe maried A Mvnday the second of March

1585 (?).

Mr Thomas Awbre and Mary Mancell maried A Mvnday the xij of February.

1586—1589

[*No entries.*]

1590

Nicholas Walter and Alse Edward maried A Thursday the last of Aprill
Richard Harry and Anne Bassett maried A Thursday the ixth of Julij
John Watkin and Jenett Thomas maried A Sonnday the xxvijth of September.
Griffith Johns and Elizabeth Bedgo^{r} (?) maried A Sonnday the xiiijth of Februarij

1591.

Myricke ap Jevan and Anne Mathew maried A Tewsday the xxvjth of October

1592

Willia' Howard and Elinor Johns maried A Twisday the viijth of Februarij

1593

[*No entries*]

1594

Edward Elis and Mary Matho maried A Sonnday the vijth of June
Willia' Matho and Ma^{r}gare Jevan maried A Sonnday the xvth of September
Thomas Bassett and Mary Bassett maried A Twisday the viijth of October
Edward Thomas and Sara Thomas maried A Saterdaye the xijth of October
Thomas John and Cissill Dawkin maried A Saterday the last of November
Lewis Dawkin and Alse Bawdrib maried A Sonday the xvjth of ffebruarij

1595

James Bassett and Katerin Johns maried A Twisday the xth of June

1596

Jevon David and Alse Morte maried A Mvnday the xijth of Aprill

159–.

Willia' Haward and Margarett Dakin maried A Saterday the first of October

1598 (?).

Anthoni Gwine and Katerin Awbre maried a Twisday the xxiiij[th] of Januarij

1599.

David Thomas and Elizabeth Haward maried A Mvnday viz the xj[th] of December
William David and Janne Deere maried A Sonnday viz the xvij[th] of June
Morgan Griffith and Katerin Dawkin maried A Sonnday viz the viij[th] of Julij
John Matho and Caterin W[m] maried A Mvndaye viz the xxiiij[th] of September
David Dawkin and Margerie John maried A Sonnday viz the vij[th] of October
George Pranch and Katerin Haward maryed A Mvnday viz the xxij[th] of October

1600.

John Niccholl and Mary Johnes were married y[e] fifte day of Nove'ber
Mathew Francis and Alis Evan were married y[e] ninthe of Nove'ber
Ricc Haward and Ann Johnes were married the 19th Januarij

1601

[*No entries*]

1602.

Thomas Prichard and Elizabeth Stephens were married the 25th day of Octob'.

1603

[*No entries*]

1604

Mathew Rosser & Mary Johnes vidua were maried the 31° day of Septe'b'.

1605

Edwardus Prichard de Lantrytheed rector et Elizabetha' Johns de eade' matrimonio erant coniuncti decimo die Julij.
Henricus Penry et Joanna' Basset matrimonio erant coniuncti 26 die Augustij
John David and Christian Richards were maried the 15th of Sept
Nest John and John Mayo were maried the 19th of May

1606.

John Howell de Lechcastell and Joan John de Lantrytheed were maried the 19 day of Maij An'o p'dict
William Dawkin & Joan Richard were maried by John Jenkin clerke curat of S[t] Tillary 18 of Jun'.

1607

Rawleins Bussie et Cicilia Mansell matrimonio erant coniuncti 16 Aprilis.

1608.

Morgan Yeavan and Catherin John Thomas were maried 22th of Maij

1609

[*No entries*]

1610

Wm Bersey & Joan Decre were maried mense Maij . .

1611.

Thomas Spencer of St Tathan and Margret Prichard were maried 28 of Octob'.

1612.

[*No entries*]

1613.

Robert Buttun gent and Jane Awbrey the daughter of Sr Thomas Awbrey Knight were maried sexto die Maij

Oliver Mathew of the p'ish of Bau . (?) and Elizab' Edward were maried 19 of Octob'.

Robert Walter of the Butt' (?) lays and Cissill Bassett the daughter of James Bassett were married 9° die Nove'b'

Edward Williams and Elizab' Bassett daughter to James Bassett were married [*no date given*]

1614.

David Jenkins Armiger et Cicilia Awbrey filia Thomæ Awbrey Militis matrimonio erant coniuncti 7° die Septemb'

Thomas Younge of Penm'ke and Ginnett Edward the daughter of Willia' Edward were maried 21 Decemb'.

1615.

[*No entries*]

1616.

Willia' Haward son to Willia' Haward deceased and An' Richard of S^t ffagans were maried 25° Junij

John ab John de Llan Dynnoodd and An' Penry of Lantrytheed were maried 9° die Decemb'.

Lewis Rice de Lancarvan and Jane Evan the daughter of Evan Thomas of Lantrytheed were maried 3° Martij

1617.

John Rice of ye parish of and Elizab' Dawkin of Lansannour were maried in the Church of Lantritheed by Edward Robinson rector of Lansannour affores^d the 29 of June.

1618

William Jenkin and Jane Thomas were maried 31° die Maij.

1619.

[*No entries*]

1620

Morgan John and Cissill Edward were maried 29° Octob'

1621.

[*No entries*]

1622

Lle'n Nicholas of the p'ish of Lanblethian and Katherin John of Lantritheed were maried 13° Maij

1623.

William Pranch and Elenor Jones were maried the 6 of August
Rice Edward and Barbra Lashbrook maried 1623 [*sic*]

1624.

John ab John and Johan Myricke were maried 2° Junij
John Dawkin and Mary Bassett were maried 26 day of Octob'

1625.

[*No entries*]

1626.

Robert Thomas and Mary Thomas were maried 24° Septemb'
Jenkin David maried to Margerett Harry Anno Dom 1626 [*sic*]

1627

Richard Jenⁿn and Eva Robin were maried 18° Junij
Thomas Mathew and Katherin Penry were maried 5° Febru'
Wm Gyllon and Elizab' Prichard were maried 20 Febru'

1628

Walter Baskerfeild Esqr and Ann Awbrey were maried 4° Decemb'

1629

Thomas Love and Mary Penry were maried the twelfe of August

1630

[*No entries*]

1631.

Harrie Robert and Cissill Penrie were maried . May

1632.

Jenkin Thomas and Elizabeth George were maried 24° Junij

1633

Jenkin Phillipp of Boulston and Elizabeth Harrie of Lantritheed were maried 13° Junij.
William John of Lancarvan and Katherin Edward were maried 8° Novemb

1634

[*No entries*]

1635.

Sr Rice Rudd Baronett was maryed to Mrs Elizabeth Awbrey the . * daye of July

1636—1638

[*No entries*]

1639

Owenus Morgan et Johanna Rosser matrimonio se^r^ coniuncti fuerunt 3^tio^ Maij
Lodovicus Williams et Cicilia Rosser matrimonio se coniuncti fuerunt 12° Maij

1640

Thomas Hopkin and Marie Williams were maried the xxx^th^ daie of May

1641—1643.

[*No entries*]

1644

Sr Nicholas Chemish Knight & Barronett and Jane Herbert wid were maried in the Church of Lantrithed the fowrth daie of November.

1645—1652.

[*No entries*]

1653

Thomas Morgan & Anne Butler married the first of June

1654—1662.

[*No entries*]

1663

William Bassette Esqr and Doctor of Lawes was maried in the Church of Llantrithyd with Mrs Margarette Button daughter of Roberte Button Esq late of Dyffryn deceased the 3 day of ffebruary

1664.

James Hugh and Elizabeth John both of Lantrithed were married the 14th day of May

1665—1668.

[*No entries*]

* Date illegible

1669

William John and Als Griffith both of this parish of Llantrithyd were married the 8th day of August

Mathew David of Welsh St Donats and Iuon Richard of this parish were married in this church the 22th day of September

1670

John Dauid of the parish of Llantrissant and Margarette Edward of the same were marryed in this church the 17th day of Aprill by licence

Thomas Rosser & Jane John both of Lantrithid were married ye 30th day of Nov ber

Will ye son of Antho ffrancis of Ystradowen & Mary Watkin ye daughter of Watkin D d of this p ish were maried the fourth of March

1671

Watkin David & Jane Morgan both of this p'ish were married ye 27th of Auguste

1672—1678

[*No entries*]

1679

Thomas Morgan of ye p ish of St Hilary & Mary Dauid of this p ish were maried September ye 28

Edward Morgan & Jennet Morgan both of this p ish were maried Feb ye 29

William Hopkin & An'e Deare both of this p'ish were married No'ber ye 10th

1680

[*No entries*]

1681

Charles Morgan & Mary Deare were married in this p'ish church May 18

Richard John & Catherin Hiet both of this parish were married May 20 (or 29) [*sic*]

Nicholas Rosser and Ellinor William both of this parish was [*sic*] maried the 13 day of November

1682, 1683

[*No entries*]

1684.

John Davies & Mary Williams was [*sic*] maried ye 26 of ffebruary

1685

[*No entries*]

1686

Edward Morgan & Margery Jenkin both of this parish were marryed ye 19th day of June

1687.

Hopkin Jenkin and Joan Dyer both of this parish were marryed June 4

1688.

Richard Harry and Joan Rosser both of this parish were married Aprill ye 16th

1689, 1690.

[*No entries*]

1691

Lewis Howell and Ann William both of this parish were marryed ye 25 day of Aprill
Thomas Edward and Wenllyan David both of this parish were married May 13th.
Lewis Aubrey Clerk and Rector of this parish was marryed to Mrs Jennett Howard spinster of the same parish ye 24th of June

1692.

[*No entries*]

1693.

Benjamin Langton and Ann Harry widdow of this parish were marryed October ye 5th
John Wilkin & Jane Jenkin both of this parish were marryed Nov 18th

1694

Roderick William of ye parish of Penmark & Lettice David of this parish were maried Dec 12.

1695.

Mr John Thomas of ye parish of St Brides & Mrs Ann Thomas widow of this parish were married Sept. 2
George Rosser & Elizabeth William both of them of this parish were married September 30th

1696

[*No entries*]

1697

John Christopher & Joan Dyer both of this parish were marryed Sept 16

1698

Morgan Harry and Cicill Jenkin were marryed the 12th of May.
Thomas Jenkin & Ann Water were marryed ye first of August
Thomas Meirick & Wenllian Walter were marryed Febr 15.

1699-1700.

William Watkin and Elizabeth Lewis were marryed the 10th of Febr

1700.

J^n Watkin & Mary Rosser were married ye 10 of May.

1701

Thomas Roberts and Elizabeth Courtney were married the 10th of December
Sr Charles Kemmyes and Dame Mary Aubrey were married the 31th of December.

1702.

William Lleysson and Margarett Robert were married the 7th of May

1703

Edward Powell Clerk and Rector of this parish was married to Mrs Catherine Lewis spinster of the same parish the 1st of June.

1703-4

Thomas Rosser and Margarett John both of this parish were married the 4th of Feb.

1704.

Edward Morgan and Mary William were married the 26th of May

1705.

William Morgan of the parish of Lantrissent and Anne Morgan of the parish of Lanedern were married the 14th of May

1706

Richard Morgan and Margarett Evan were married the 26th of 9^ber

1707, 1708
[*No entries*]

1709.

Edward Lewis & Elenor Miles were maried May 1
Walter Howell & Margarett Philip of ye p^rish of St John near Cardiff were married Sept 29°

1710

Henry Philip & Jane William both of this parish were married Aug^st 4°.

1711—1714.
[*No entries*]

1715

Evan Rees & Jennett Evan were married May 1st
Morgan Rees & Catherine [*sic*].

1716

Samuel Williams & Magdalen Dawkins were married June 7th

1717

Henry Richard & Joan Williams were married Feb 17th

1718, 1719.

[*No entries*]

1720

Thomas David & Katherine Richard both of this p'ish were married Febry 6th

1721.

[*No entries*]

1722

Philip David & Anne William were married Feb 5th
Howell John of Cowbridge & Eliz Walter of this p'ish were married Oct 19th

1723.

John William & Mary James both of this p'ish were maried Janry 29th

1724—1726.

[*No entries*]

1727.

Lewis John of ye parish of Bonuilstowne and Jane John of this parish were maried May ye 19th
Christopher Courtney and Joane Jenkin both of this parish were maried Augst ye 19th

1727-8

Samuel Watkins of ye parish of Welsh St Dunats and Catherin Dauid of Lancaruan wear maried Feb ye 19th

1728.

James Robert of ye parish of Welsh St Donats and Ann Lewis of ye parish of Lantrissent were married May ye 13th
Morgan Euan and Cicill Hugh both of this parish wear maried 9ber ye 6th

1729

[*No entries*]

1730

Thomas Thomas and Catherin Griffith wear maried May ye 7

1731

Isack and Anne Christopher wear maried July ye 31th

1732

[*No entries*]

1733-4

William David & Jane Edward were married Febr 5
Christopher Courtney and Sara Reese both of this psh was [*sic*] maried ye 23 of Febr
John Robert and Anne Jones of ye parish of Pemarck were maried hear Febrewary ye 24

1734

Robert Lougher and Margaret Hugh of the parish of St Hillery wear maried here August ye 17

1735

Lewelin Euan of the parish of Lantrissant and Margaret Hendry of this parish wear maried hear July the 28

1735-6

Thomas Walters & Eleanor Watts the former of the parish of St Athan ye latter of ye parish of Gileston were married ye 10th of Febr.
Edwd Jenkin of ye parish of Covty & Catherine Mathew of ye parish of Penmark were married ye 2d day of March

1736—1738

[*No entries*]

1739.

John Christopher and Jane John both of this parish were married May 11
Harry John and Mary David both of this parish were married May 18.
David William and Mary John both of this parish were married June 11th
William Morgan of this parish and Dorothy John of the parish of Lancarvan were married January 5.

1740.

Miles Thomas of the parish of Welch St Donats and Margaret Lewis of the same were married July 27

1741—1743

[*No entries*]

1744

Watkin Thomas of ye parish of Lansanfread & Ann Millward of this parish were married Octr 29th
Thomas Cook & Elizabeth Jenkin both of this parish were married Feby 23d

1745

John Hicks of ye parish of Bonvilston & Elizabeth Thomas of this parish were married Octr ye 10th.

1746.

Jenkin John of the parish of Pendoylon and Mary Thomas of this parish were married Feby 27th

1747.

John Thomas of the parish of Lancarvan and Margaret Edward of this parish were married Augt 27th.

1748

John March & Mary Morgan both of this parish were married Ap 23
Richard Thomas and Esther David both of this parish were married Decr 26th

1749.

Edward Lewis and Margaret Thomas both of this parish were married May 29th.
Thomas Robert of the parish of St Mary Hill & Catherine Llewellin of the parish of Pile were married Feby 14th.

1750.

John Lewis of the parish of Lancarvan and Jennet Christopher of this parish were married June 24th
John Hornal and Anne Powell both of this parish were married Sepr 1st
David Griffith and Mary John both of this parish were married Decr 3^d^.

1751.

David Jones of the parish of St Hillary and Jane Jones of this parish were married May 9th

1752.

Thomas Morgan and Joan Thomas both of this parish were married June 18

MEMORANDA.

May 27, 1685

Memorandum that on the day and in the year above set down, The Minister Churchwardens and others of the parishioners of Lantrithid with a convenient number of boyes took from the school for that purpose went on procession around the whole parish, examining the fines bounds & limitations of the said parish, according to an Antient and usefull Custom, and instructing the boyes where they lay that they might be sure to remember them, that being able hereby to give an account of the just extent of their own they may ever maintain it, neither offering any wrong to nor taking any from other adjacent parishes

L. Aubrey Rector

The names of all the boyes whom we took with us in our perambulation

Robert the son of John Robert clerk of this parish
William the son of William John of the same parish
Christopher the son of Anth: Rees of the same parish
David the son of Christopher Scipio of the same
George the son of Watkin David of the same
Christopher the son of Mary Watkin of the same

May ye 15, 1702

Memorandum that on the day and in the year above set down, The Minister and other Parishioners of Lantrithyd with a convenient number of Boys went on Procession around the whole Parish, examining the fines, bounds and Limitations of the said parish, according to an Antient and usefull Custom, and instructing the Boys where they lay, that they may be sure to remember them, that being able thereby to give an account of the just extent of their own they may ever maintain it, neither offering any wrong to nor taking any from other adjacent Parishes

Ed: Powell Rector

The Minister & Church-warden &c. went on procession around ye Parish of Lantrythyd on Holy Thursday & Whitsun-Tuesday in ye year 1718.

Wm Hopkins Rectr

The young men & youths' names who accompanied ye Procession:

Wm Dawkin, John Griffith, Thomas David, Jenkin Dawkin, Thomas John, Thom. Watkin, Wm John.

The Minister & Church-warden &c. went on procession around the Parish of Lantrithyd on Easter Monday in the year 1747.

N Hopkins Rector.

The young men & youths' names who accompanied the Procession:

Robert Savours, John Thomas, Isaac David, John Christopher, Lewis Howell—Edwd Samuel, Charles & George Evan, Evan David, Richard Lewis.

INDEX.

E

F

G

H

J

K

L

Y

London Mitchell and Hughes, Printers, 140 Wardour Street, W

Lightning Source UK Ltd.
Milton Keynes UK
UKHW021821170321
380525UK00006B/1488